PYTHON

BASIC TUTORIALS

LEARN PYTHON PROGRAMMING LANGUAGE
FROM THE SCRATCH

ADNEY AINSLEY

PYTHON - TUTORIAL

Python is a general-purpose interpreted, interactive, object-oriented, and high-level programming language. It was created by Guido van Rossum during 1985- 1990. Like Perl, Python source code is also available under the GNU General Public License (GPL). This tutorial gives enough understanding on Python programming language.

AUDIENCE

This tutorial is designed for software programmers who need to learn Python programming language from scratch.

PREREQUISITES

You should have a basic understanding of Computer Programming terminologies. A basic understanding of any of the programming languages is a plus.

TABLE OF CONTENTS

PYTHON OVERVIEW

Python is a high-level, interpreted, interactive and object-oriented scripting language. Python is designed to be highly readable. It uses English keywords frequently where as other languages use punctuation, and it has fewer syntactical constructions than other languages.

- Python is Interpreted — Python is processed at runtime by the interpreter. You do not need to compile your program before executing it. This is similar to PERL and PHP.

- Python is Interactive — You can actually sit at a Python prompt and interact with the interpreter directly to write your programs.

- Python is Object-Oriented — Python supports Object-Oriented style or technique of programming that encapsulates code within objects.

- Python is a Beginner's Language — Python is a great language for the beginner-level programmers and supports the development of a wide range of applications from simple text processing to WWW browsers to games.

HISTORY OF PYTHON

Python was developed by Guido van Rossum in the late eighties and early nineties at the National Research Institute for Mathematics and Computer Science in the Netherlands.

Python is derived from many other languages, including ABC, Modula-3, C, C++, Algol-68, SmallTalk, and Unix shell and other scripting languages.

Python is copyrighted. Like Perl, Python source code is now available under the GNU General Public License (GPL).

Python is now maintained by a core development team at the institute, although Guido van Rossum still holds a vital role in directing its progress.

PYTHON FEATURES

Python's features include —

- Easy-to-learn — Python has few keywords, simple structure, and a clearly defined syntax. This allows the student to pick up the language quickly.

- Easy-to-read — Python code is more clearly defined and visible to the eyes.

- Easy-to-maintain — Python's source code is fairly easy-to-maintain.

- A broad standard library — Python's bulk of the library is very portable and cross-platform compatible on UNIX, Windows, and Macintosh.

- Interactive Mode — Python has support for an interactive mode which allows interactive testing and debugging of snippets of code.

- Portable — Python can run on a wide variety of hardware platforms and has the same interface on all platforms.

- Extendable — You can add low-level modules to the Python interpreter. These modules enable programmers to add to or customize their tools to be more efficient.

- Databases — Python provides interfaces to all major commercial databases.

- GUI Programming — Python supports GUI applications that can be created and ported to many system calls, libraries and windows systems, such as Windows MFC, Macintosh, and the X Window system of Unix.

- Scalable — Python provides a better structure and support for large programs than shell scripting.

2

- Apart from the above-mentioned features, Python has a big list of good features, few are listed below –

- It supports functional and structured programming methods as well as OOP.

- It can be used as a scripting language or can be compiled to byte-code for building large applications.

- It provides very high-level dynamic data types and supports dynamic type checking.

- IT supports automatic garbage collection.

- It can be easily integrated with C, C++, COM, ActiveX, CORBA, and Java.

PYTHON - ENVIRONMENT SETUP

Python is available on a wide variety of platforms including Linux and Mac OS X. Let's understand how to set up our Python environment.

LOCAL ENVIRONMENT SETUP

Open a terminal window and type "python" to find out if it is already installed and which version is installed.

- Unix (Solaris, Linux, FreeBSD, AIX, HP/UX, SunOS, IRIX, etc.)
- Win 9x/NT/2000
- Macintosh (Intel, PPC, 68K)
- OS/2
- DOS (multiple versions)
- PalmOS
- Nokia mobile phones
- Windows CE
- Acorn/RISC OS
- BeOS
- Amiga
- VMS/OpenVMS
- QNX
- VxWorks
- Psion
- Python has also been ported to the Java and .NET virtual machines
-

4

GETTING PYTHON

The most up-to-date and current source code, binaries, documentation, news, etc., is available on the official website of Python https://www.python.org/

You can download Python documentation from https://www.python.org/doc/. The documentation is available in HTML, PDF, and PostScript formats.

INSTALLING PYTHON

Python distribution is available for a wide variety of platforms. You need to download only the binary code applicable for your platform and install Python.

If the binary code for your platform is not available, you need a C compiler to compile the source code manually. Compiling the source code offers more flexibility in terms of choice of features that you require in your installation.

Here is a quick overview of installing Python on various platforms –

UNIX AND LINUX INSTALLATION

Here are the simple steps to install Python on Unix/Linux machine.

- Open a Web browser and go to https://www.python.org/downloads/.
- Follow the link to download zipped source code available for Unix/Linux.
- Download and extract files.
- Editing the *Modules/Setup* file if you want to customize some options.
- run ./configure script

- make
- make install
- This installs Python at standard location */usr/local/bin* and its libraries at */usr/local/lib/pythonXX* where XX is the version of Python.

WINDOWS INSTALLATION

Here are the steps to install Python on Windows machine.

- Open a Web browser and go to https://www.python.org/downloads/.
- Follow the link for the Windows installer *python-XYZ.msi* file where XYZ is the version you need to install.
- To use this installer *python-XYZ.msi*, the Windows system must support Microsoft Installer 2.0. Save the installer file to your local machine and then run it to find out if your machine supports MSI.
- Run the downloaded file. This brings up the Python install wizard, which is really easy to use. Just accept the default settings, wait until the install is finished, and you are done.

MACINTOSH INSTALLATION

Recent Macs come with Python installed, but it may be several years out of date. See http://www.python.org/download/mac/ for instructions on getting the current version along with extra tools to support development on the Mac. For older Mac OS's before Mac OS X 10.3 (released in 2003), MacPython is available.

Jack Jansen maintains it and you can have full access to the entire documentation at his website – http://www.cwi.nl/~jack/macpython.html. You can find complete installation details for Mac OS installation.

Setting up PATH

Programs and other executable files can be in many directories, so operating systems provide a search path that lists the directories that the OS searches for executables.

The path is stored in an environment variable, which is a named string maintained by the operating system. This variable contains information available to the command shell and other programs.

The path variable is named as PATH in Unix or Path in Windows (Unix is case sensitive; Windows is not).

In Mac OS, the installer handles the path details. To invoke the Python interpreter from any particular directory, you must add the Python directory to your path.

Setting path at Unix/Linux

To add the Python directory to the path for a particular session in Unix –

- In the csh shell – type setenv PATH "$PATH:/usr/local/bin/python" and press Enter.

- In the bash shell (Linux) – type export ATH="$PATH:/usr/local/bin/python" and press Enter.

- In the sh or ksh shell – type PATH="$PATH:/usr/local/bin/python" and press Enter.

- Note – /usr/local/bin/python is the path of the Python directory

SETTING PATH AT WINDOWS

To add the Python directory to the path for a particular session in Windows −

At the command prompt − type path %path%;C:\Python and press Enter.

Note − C:\Python is the path of the Python directory

PYTHON ENVIRONMENT VÀRIABLES

Here are important environment variables, which can be recognized by Python –

Sr.No.	Variable & Description
1	**PYTHONPATH** It has a role similar to PATH. This variable tells the Python interpreter where to locate the module files imported into a program. It should include the Python source library directory and the directories containing Python source code. PYTHONPATH is sometimes preset by the Python installer.
2	**PYTHONSTARTUP** It contains the path of an initialization file containing Python source code. It is executed every time you start the interpreter. It is named as .pythonrc.py in Unix and it contains commands that load utilities or modify PYTHONPATH.
3	**PYTHONCASEOK** It is used in Windows to instruct Python to find the first case-insensitive match in an import statement. Set this variable to any value to activate it.
4	**PYTHONHOME** It is an alternative module search path. It is usually embedded in the PYTHONSTARTUP or PYTHONPATH directories to make switching module libraries easy.

RUNNING PYTHON

There are three different ways to start Python –

INTERACTIVE INTERPRETER

You can start Python from Unix, DOS, or any other system that provides you a command-line interpreter or shell window.

Enter python the command line.

Start coding right away in the interactive interpreter.

```
$python # Unix/Linux
or
python% # Unix/Linux
or
C:> python # Windows/DOS
```

Here is the list of all the available command line options –

Sr.No.	Option & Description
1	**-d** It provides debug output.
2	**-O** It generates optimized bytecode (resulting in .pyo files).
3	**-S** Do not run import site to look for Python paths on startup.
4	**-v** verbose output (detailed trace on import statements).
5	**-X** disable class-based built-in exceptions (just use strings); obsolete starting with version 1.6.
6	**-c cmd** run Python script sent in as cmd string
7	**file** run Python script from given file

SCRIPT FROM THE COMMAND-LINE

A Python script can be executed at command line by invoking the interpreter on your application, as in the following –

```
$python script.py # Unix/Linux
or

python% script.py # Unix/Linux
or

C: >python script.py # Windows/DOS
```
Note – Be sure the file permission mode allows execution.

INTEGRATED DEVELOPMENT ENVIRONMENT

You can run Python from a Graphical User Interface (GUI) environment as well, if you have a GUI application on your system that supports Python.

- Unix – IDLE is the very first Unix IDE for Python.
- Windows – PythonWin is the first Windows interface for Python and is an IDE with a GUI.
- Macintosh – The Macintosh version of Python along with the IDLE IDE is available from the main website, downloadable as either MacBinary or BinHex'd files.

If you are not able to set up the environment properly, then you can take help from your system admin. Make sure the Python environment is properly set up and working perfectly fine.

Note – All the examples given in subsequent chapters are executed with Python 2.4.3 version available on CentOS flavor of Linux.

We already have set up Python Programming environment online, so that you can execute all the available examples online at the same time when you are learning theory. Feel free to modify any example and execute it online.

PYTHON - BASIC SYNTAX

The Python language has many similarities to Perl, C, and Java. However, there are some definite differences between the languages.

FIRST PYTHON PROGRAM

Let us execute programs in different modes of programming.

INTERACTIVE MODE PROGRAMMING

Invoking the interpreter without passing a script file as a parameter brings up the following prompt —

```
$ python
Python 2.4.3 (#1, Nov 11 2010, 13:34:43)
[GCC 4.1.2 20080704 (Red Hat 4.1.2-48)] on linux2
Type "help", "copyright", "credits" or "license" for more
information.
>>>
```

Type the following text at the Python prompt and press the Enter —

```
>>> print "Hello, Python!"
```

If you are running new version of Python, then you would need to use print statement with parenthesis as in print ("Hello, Python!");. However in Python version 2.4.3, this produces the following result —

```
Hello, Python!
```

Script Mode Programming

Invoking the interpreter with a script parameter begins execution of the script and continues until the script is finished. When the script is finished, the interpreter is no longer active.

Let us write a simple Python program in a script. Python files have extension .py. Type the following source code in a test.py file -

```
print "Hello, Python!"
```

We assume that you have Python interpreter set in PATH variable. Now, try to run this program as follows —

```
$ python test.py
```

This produces the following result —

```
Hello, Python!
```

Let us try another way to execute a Python script. Here is the modified test.py file —

```
#!/usr/bin/python
```

```
print "Hello, Python!"
```

We assume that you have Python interpreter available in /usr/bin directory. Now, try to run this program as follows —

```
$ chmod +x test.py      # This is to make file executable
$./test.py
```

This produces the following result —

```
Hello, Python!
```

PYTHON IDENTIFIERS

A Python identifier is a name used to identify a variable, function, class, module or other object. An identifier starts with a letter A to Z or a to z or an underscore (_) followed by zero or more letters, underscores and digits (0 to 9).

Python does not allow punctuation characters such as @, $, and % within identifiers. Python is a case sensitive programming language. Thus, Manpower and manpower are two different identifiers in Python.

Here are naming conventions for Python identifiers –

- Class names start with an uppercase letter. All other identifiers start with a lowercase letter.
- Starting an identifier with a single leading underscore indicates that the identifier is private.
- Starting an identifier with two leading underscores indicates a strongly private identifier.
- If the identifier also ends with two trailing underscores, the identifier is a language-defined special name.

RESERVED WORDS

The following list shows the Python keywords. These are reserved words and you cannot use them as constant or variable or any other identifier names. All the Python keywords contain lowercase letters only.

and	exec	not
assert	finally	or
break	for	pass
class	from	print
continue	global	raise
def	if	return
del	import	try
elif	in	while
else	is	with
except	lambda	yield

LINES AND INDENTATION

Python provides no braces to indicate blocks of code for class and function definitions or flow control. Blocks of code are denoted by line indentation, which is rigidly enforced.

The number of spaces in the indentation is variable, but all statements within the block must be indented the same amount. For example –

```
if True:
    print "True"
else:
    print "False"
```

However, the following block generates an error –

```
if True:
    print "Answer"
    print "True"
else:
    print "Answer"
    print "False"
```

Thus, in Python all the continuous lines indented with same number of spaces would form a block. The following example has various statement blocks –

Note – Do not try to understand the logic at this point of time. Just make sure you understood various blocks even if they are without braces.

```
#!/usr/bin/python

import sys

try:
    # open file stream
    file = open(file_name, "w")
except IOError:
    print "There was an error writing to", file_name
    sys.exit()
```

```
print "Enter '", file_finish,
print "' When finished"
while file_text != file_finish:
    file_text = raw_input("Enter text: ")
    if file_text == file_finish:
        # close the file
        file.close
        break
    file.write(file_text)
    file.write("\n")
file.close()
file_name = raw_input("Enter filename: ")
if len(file_name) == 0:
    print "Next time please enter something"
    sys.exit()
try:
    file = open(file_name, "r")
except IOError:
    print "There was an error reading file"
    sys.exit()
file_text = file.read()
file.close()
print file_text
```

MULTI-LINE STATEMENTS

Statements in Python typically end with a new line. Python does, however, allow the use of the line continuation character (\) to denote that the line should continue. For example –

```
total = item_one + \
        item_two + \
        item_three
```

Statements contained within the [], {}, or () brackets do not need to use the line continuation character. For example –

```
days = ['Monday', 'Tuesday', 'Wednesday',
        'Thursday', 'Friday']
```

QUOTATION IN PYTHON

Python accepts single ('), double (") and triple (''' or """) quotes to denote string literals, as long as the same type of quote starts and ends the string.

The triple quotes are used to span the string across multiple lines. For example, all the following are legal —

```
word = 'word'
sentence = "This is a sentence."
paragraph = """This is a paragraph. It is
made up of multiple lines and sentences."""
```

COMMENTS IN PYTHON

A hash sign (#) that is not inside a string literal begins a comment. All characters after the # and up to the end of the physical line are part of the comment and the Python interpreter ignores them.

```
#!/usr/bin/python
```

```
# First comment
print "Hello, Python!" # second comment
```

This produces the following result –

```
Hello, Python!
```

You can type a comment on the same line after a statement or expression —

```
name = "Madisetti" # This is again comment
```

You can comment multiple lines as follows –

```
# This is a comment.
# This is a comment, too.
# This is a comment, too.
# I said that already.
```

USING BLANK LINES

A line containing only whitespace, possibly with a comment, is known as a blank line and Python totally ignores it.

In an interactive interpreter session, you must enter an empty physical line to terminate a multiline statement.

WAITING FOR THE USER

The following line of the program displays the prompt, the statement saying "Press the enter key to exit", and waits for the user to take action –

```
#!/usr/bin/python

raw_input("\n\nPress the enter key to exit.")
```

Here, "\n\n" is used to create two new lines before displaying the actual line. Once the user presses the key, the program ends. This is a nice trick to keep a console window open until the user is done with an application.

MULTIPLE STATEMENTS ON A SINGLE LINE

The semicolon (;) allows multiple statements on the single line given that neither statement starts a new code block. Here is a sample snip using the semicolon −

```
import sys; x = 'foo'; sys.stdout.write(x + '\n')
```

MULTIPLE STATEMENT GROUPS AS SUITES

A group of individual statements, which make a single code block are called suites in Python. Compound or complex statements, such as if, while, def, and class require a header line and a suite.

Header lines begin the statement (with the keyword) and terminate with a colon (:) and are followed by one or more lines which make up the suite.

For example −

```
if expression :
    suite
elif expression :
    suite
else :
    suite
```

COMMAND LINE ARGUMENTS

Many programs can be run to provide you with some basic information about how they should be run. Python enables you to do this with -h —

```
$ python -h
usage: python [option] ... [-c cmd | -m mod | file | -] [arg] ...
Options and arguments (and corresponding environment variables):
-c cmd : program passed in as string (terminates option list)
-d     : debug output from parser (also PYTHONDEBUG=x)
-E     : ignore environment variables (such as PYTHONPATH)
-h     : print this help message and exit

[ etc. ]
```

You can also program your script in such a way that it should accept various options.

PYTHON - VARIABLE TYPES

Variables are nothing but reserved memory locations to store values. This means that when you create a variable you reserve some space in memory.

Based on the data type of a variable, the interpreter allocates memory and decides what can be stored in the reserved memory. Therefore, by assigning different data types to variables, you can store integers, decimals or characters in these variables.

ASSIGNING VALUES TO VARIABLES

Python variables do not need explicit declaration to reserve memory space. The declaration happens automatically when you assign a value to a variable. The equal sign (=) is used to assign values to variables.

The operand to the left of the = operator is the name of the variable and the operand to the right of the = operator is the value stored in the variable. For example −

```
#!/usr/bin/python
counter = 100          # An integer assignment
miles   = 1000.0       # A floating point
name    = "John"       # A string
print counter
print miles
print name
```

Here, 100, 1000.0 and "John" are the values assigned to counter, miles, and name variables, respectively. This produces the following result −

```
100
1000.0
John
```

MULTIPLE ASSIGNMENT

Python allows you to assign a single value to several variables simultaneously. For example –

```
a = b = c = 1
```

Here, an integer object is created with the value 1, and all three variables are assigned to the same memory location. You can also assign multiple objects to multiple variables. For example –

```
a,b,c = 1,2,"john"
```

Here, two integer objects with values 1 and 2 are assigned to variables a and b respectively, and one string object with the value "john" is assigned to the variable c.

STANDARD DATA TYPES

The data stored in memory can be of many types. For example, a person's age is stored as a numeric value and his or her address is stored as alphanumeric characters. Python has various standard data types that are used to define the operations possible on them and the storage method for each of them.

Python has five standard data types –

- Numbers
- String
- List
- Tuple
- Dictionary

PYTHON NUMBERS

Number data types store numeric values. Number objects are created when you assign a value to them. For example —

```
var1 = 1
var2 = 10
```

You can also delete the reference to a number object by using the del statement. The syntax of the del statement is —

```
del var1[,var2[,var3[....,varN]]]]
```

You can delete a single object or multiple objects by using the del statement. For example —

```
del var
del var_a, var_b
```

Python supports four different numerical types —

- int (signed integers)
- long (long integers, they can also be represented in octal and hexadecimal)
- float (floating point real values)
- complex (complex numbers)

EXAMPLES

Here are some examples of numbers –

int	long	float	complex
10	51924361L	0.0	3.14j
100	-0x19323L	15.20	45.j
-786	0122L	-21.9	9.322e-36j
080	0xDEFABCECBDAECBFBAEl	32.3+e18	.876j
-0490	535633629843L	-90.	-.6545+0J
-0x260	-052318172735L	-32.54e100	3e+26J
0x69	-4721885298529L	70.2-E12	4.53e-7j

- Python allows you to use a lowercase l with long, but it is recommended that you use only an uppercase L to avoid confusion with the number 1. Python displays long integers with an uppercase L.

- A complex number consists of an ordered pair of real floating-point numbers denoted by x + yj, where x and y are the real numbers and j is the imaginary unit.

PYTHON STRINGS

Strings in Python are identified as a contiguous set of characters represented in the quotation marks. Python allows for either pairs of single or double quotes. Subsets of strings can be taken using the slice operator ([ ] and [:]) with indexes starting at 0 in the beginning of the string and working their way from -1 at the end.

The plus (+) sign is the string concatenation operator and the asterisk (*) is the repetition operator. For example −

```
#!/usr/bin/python

str = 'Hello World!'

print str          # Prints complete string
print str[0]       # Prints first character of the string
print str[2:5]     # Prints characters starting from 3rd to 5th
print str[2:]      # Prints string starting from 3rd character
print str * 2      # Prints string two times
print str + "TEST" # Prints concatenated string
```

This will produce the following result −

```
Hello World!
H
llo
llo World!
Hello World!Hello World!
Hello World!TEST
```

PYTHON LISTS

Lists are the most versatile of Python's compound data types. A list contains items separated by commas and enclosed within square brackets ([]). To some extent, lists are similar to arrays in C. One difference between them is that all the items belonging to a list can be of different data type.

The values stored in a list can be accessed using the slice operator ([ ] and [:]) with indexes starting at 0 in the beginning of the list and working their way to end -1. The plus (+) sign is the list concatenation operator, and the asterisk (*) is the repetition operator. For example −

```
#!/usr/bin/python

list = [ 'abcd', 786 , 2.23, 'john', 70.2 ]
tinylist = [123, 'john']

print list            # Prints complete list
print list[0]         # Prints first element of the list
print list[1:3]       # Prints elements starting from 2nd till 4th
print list[2:]        # Prints elements starting from 3rd element
print tinylist * 2    # Prints list two times
print list + tinylist # Prints concatenated lists
```

This produce the following result −

```
['abcd', 786, 2.23, 'john', 70.200000000000003]
abcd
[786, 2.23]
[2.23, 'john', 70.200000000000003]
[123, 'john', 123, 'john']
['abcd', 786, 2.23, 'john', 70.200000000000003, 123, 'john']
```

PYTHON TUPLES

A tuple is another sequence data type that is similar to the list. A tuple consists of a number of values separated by commas. Unlike lists, however, tuples are enclosed within parentheses.

The main differences between lists and tuples are: Lists are enclosed in brackets ([ ]) and their elements and size can be changed, while tuples are enclosed in parentheses (( )) and cannot be updated. Tuples can be thought of as read-only lists. For example −

```
#!/usr/bin/python


tuple = ( 'abcd', 786 , 2.23, 'john', 70.2  )
tinytuple = (123, 'john')


print tuple          # Prints complete list
print tuple[0]       # Prints first element of the list
print tuple[1:3]     # Prints elements starting from 2nd till 3rd
print tuple[2:]      # Prints elements starting from 3rd element
print tinytuple * 2  # Prints list two times
print tuple + tinytuple # Prints concatenated lists
```

This produce the following result −

```
('abcd', 786, 2.23, 'john', 70.200000000000003)
abcd
(786, 2.23)
(2.23, 'john', 70.200000000000003)
(123, 'john', 123, 'john')
('abcd', 786, 2.23, 'john', 70.200000000000003, 123, 'john')
```

The following code is invalid with tuple, because we attempted to update a tuple, which is not allowed. Similar case is possible with lists −

```
#!/usr/bin/python


tuple = ( 'abcd', 786 , 2.23, 'john', 70.2  )
list = [ 'abcd', 786 , 2.23, 'john', 70.2  ]
```

30

```
tuple[2] = 1000      # Invalid syntax with tuple
list[2] = 1000       # Valid syntax with list
```

PYTHON DICTIONARY

Python's dictionaries are kind of hash table type. They work like associative arrays or hashes found in Perl and consist of key-value pairs. A dictionary key can be almost any Python type, but are usually numbers or strings. Values, on the other hand, can be any arbitrary Python object.

Dictionaries are enclosed by curly braces ({ }) and values can be assigned and accessed using square braces ([]). For example −

```
#!/usr/bin/python

dict = {}
dict['one'] = "This is one"
dict[2]      = "This is two"

tinydict = {'name': 'john','code':6734, 'dept': 'sales'}


print dict['one']       # Prints value for 'one' key
print dict[2]           # Prints value for 2 key
print tinydict          # Prints complete dictionary
print tinydict.keys()   # Prints all the keys
print tinydict.values() # Prints all the values
```

This produce the following result −

```
This is one
This is two
{'dept': 'sales', 'code': 6734, 'name': 'john'}
['dept', 'code', 'name']
['sales', 6734, 'john']
```

Dictionaries have no concept of order among elements. It is incorrect to say that the elements are "out of order"; they are simply unordere

DATA TYPE CONVERSION

Sometimes, you may need to perform conversions between the built-in types. To convert between types, you simply use the type name as a function.

There are several built-in functions to perform conversion from one data type to another. These functions return a new object representing the converted value.

Sr.No.	Function & Description
1	**int(x [,base])** Converts x to an integer. base specifies the base if x is a string.
2	**long(x [,base])** Converts x to a long integer. base specifies the base if x is a string.
3	**float(x)** Converts x to a floating-point number.
4	**complex(real [,imag])** Creates a complex number.

5   **str(x)**

Converts object x to a string representation.

6   **repr(x)**

Converts object x to an expression string.

7   **eval(str)**

Evaluates a string and returns an object.

8   **tuple(s)**

Converts s to a tuple.

9   **list(s)**

Converts s to a list.

10   **set(s)**

Converts s to a set.

11   **dict(d)**

Creates a dictionary. d must be a sequence of (key,value) tuples.

12	**frozenset(s)** Converts s to a frozen set.
13	**chr(x)** Converts an integer to a character.
14	**unichr(x)** Converts an integer to a Unicode character.
15	**ord(x)** Converts a single character to its integer value.
16	**hex(x)** Converts an integer to a hexadecimal string.
17	**oct(x)** Converts an integer to an octal string.

Python - Basic Operators

Operators are the constructs which can manipulate the value of operands.

Consider the expression 4 + 5 = 9. Here, 4 and 5 are called operands and + is called operator.

Types of Operator

Python language supports the following types of operators.

- Arithmetic Operators
- Comparison (Relational) Operators
- Assignment Operators
- Logical Operators
- Bitwise Operators
- Membership Operators
- Identity Operators

Let us have a look on all operators one by one.

Python Arithmetic Operators

Assume variable a holds 10 and variable b holds 20, then −

Operator	Description	Example
+ Addition	Adds values on either side of the operator.	a + b = 30
- Subtraction	Subtracts right hand operand from left hand operand.	a − b = -10
* Multiplication	Multiplies values on either side of the operator	a * b = 200
/ Division	Divides left hand operand by right hand operand	b / a = 2
% Modulus	Divides left hand operand by right hand operand and returns remainder	b % a = 0
** Exponent	Performs exponential (power) calculation on operators	a**b =10 to the power 20

| // | Floor Division - The division of operands where the result is the quotient in which the digits after the decimal point are removed. But if one of the operands is negative, the result is floored, i.e., rounded away from zero (towards negative infinity) | 9//2 = 4 and 9.0//2.0 = 4.0, -11//3 = -4, -11.0//3 = -4.0 |

PYTHON COMPARISON OPERATORS

These operators compare the values on either sides of them and decide the relation among them. They are also called Relational operators.

Assume variable a holds 10 and variable b holds 20, then −

Operator	Description	Example
==	If the values of two operands are equal, then the condition becomes true.	(a == b) is not true.
!=	If values of two operands are not equal, then condition becomes true.	(a != b) is true.
<>	If values of two operands are not equal, then condition becomes true.	(a <> b) is true. This is similar to != operator.
>	If the value of left operand is greater than the value of right operand, then condition becomes true.	(a > b) is not true.
<	If the value of left operand is less than the value of right operand, then condition becomes true.	(a < b) is true.
>=	If the value of left operand is greater than or equal to the value of right operand, then condition becomes true.	(a >= b) is not true.
<=	If the value of left operand is less than or equal to the value of right operand, then condition becomes true.	(a <= b) is true.

PYTHON ASSIGNMENT OPERATORS

Assume variable a holds 10 and variable b holds 20, then −

Operator	Description	Example
=	Assigns values from right side operands to left side operand	c = a + b assigns value of a + b into c
+= Add AND	It adds right operand to the left operand and assign the result to left operand	c += a is equivalent to c = c + a
-= Subtract AND	It subtracts right operand from the left operand and assign the result to left operand	c -= a is equivalent to c = c - a
*= Multiply AND	It multiplies right operand with the left operand and assign the result to left operand	c *= a is equivalent to c = c * a
/= Divide AND	It divides left operand with the right operand and assign the result to left operand	c /= a is equivalent to c = c / ac /= a is equivalent to c = c / a

%= Modulus AND	It takes modulus using two operands and assign the result to left operand	c %= a is equivalent to c = c % a
**= Exponent AND	Performs exponential (power) calculation on operators and assign value to the left operand	c **= a is equivalent to c = c ** a
//= Floor Division	It performs floor division on operators and assign value to the left operand	c //= a is equivalent to c = c // a

PYTHON BITWISE OPERATORS

Bitwise operator works on bits and performs bit by bit operation. Assume if a = 60; and b = 13; Now in binary format they will be as follows —

a = 0011 1100

b = 0000 1101

----

a&b = 0000 1100

a|b = 0011 1101

a^b = 0011 0001

~a = 1100 0011

There are following Bitwise operators supported by Python language

Operator	Description	Example
& Binary AND	Operator copies a bit to the result if it exists in both operands	(a & b) (means 0000 1100)
| Binary OR	It copies a bit if it exists in either operand.	(a | b) = 61 (means 0011 1101)
^ Binary XOR	It copies the bit if it is set in one operand but not both.	(a ^ b) = 49 (means 0011 0001)
~ Binary Ones Complement	It is unary and has the effect of 'flipping' bits.	(~a) = -61 (means 1100 0011 in 2's complement form due to a signed binary number.
<< Binary Left Shift	The left operands value is moved left by the number of bits specified by the right operand.	a << 2 = 240 (means 1111 0000)
>> Binary Right Shift	The left operands value is moved right by the number of bits specified by the right operand.	a >> 2 = 15 (means 0000 1111)

PYTHON LOGICAL OPERATORS

There are following logical operators supported by Python language. Assume variable a holds 10 and variable b holds 20 then

Used to reverse the logical state of its operand.

PYTHON MEMBERSHIP OPERATORS

Python's membership operators test for membership in a sequence, such as strings, lists, or tuples. There are two membership operators as explained below −

Operator	Description	Example
in	Evaluates to true if it finds a variable in the specified sequence and false otherwise.	x in y, here in results in a 1 if x is a member of sequence y.
not in	Evaluates to true if it does not finds a variable in the specified sequence and false otherwise.	x not in y, here not in results in a 1 if x is not a member of sequence y.

PYTHON IDENTITY OPERATORS

Identity operators compare the memory locations of two objects. There are two Identity operators explained below –

Operator	Description	Example
is	Evaluates to true if the variables on either side of the operator point to the same object and false otherwise.	x is y, here **is** results in 1 if id(x) equals id(y).
is not	Evaluates to false if the variables on either side of the operator point to the same object and true otherwise.	x is not y, here **is not** results in 1 if id(x) is not equal to id(y).

PYTHON OPERATORS PRECEDENCE

The following table lists all operators from highest precedence to lowest.

Sr.No.	Operator & Description
1	** Exponentiation (raise to the power)
2	~ + - Complement, unary plus and minus (method names for the last two are +@ and -@)
3	* / % // Multiply, divide, modulo and floor division
4	+ - Addition and subtraction
5	>> << Right and left bitwise shift
6	& Bitwise 'AND'

7   ^ |

Bitwise exclusive `OR' and regular `OR'

8   <= < > >=

Comparison operators

9   <> == !=

Equality operators

10   = %= /= //= -= += *= **=

Assignment operators

11   is is not

Identity operators

12   in not in

Membership operators

13   not or and

Logical operators

PYTHON - DECISION MAKING

Decision making is anticipation of conditions occurring while execution of the program and specifying actions taken according to the conditions.

Decision structures evaluate multiple expressions which produce TRUE or FALSE as outcome. You need to determine which action to take and which statements to execute if outcome is TRUE or FALSE otherwise.

Following is the general form of a typical decision making structure found in most of the programming languages —

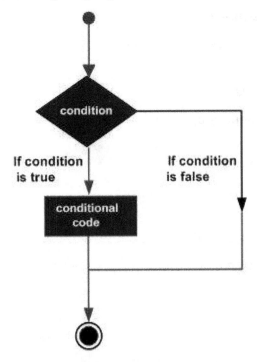

Python programming language assumes any non-zero and non-null values as TRUE, and if it is either zero or null, then it is assumed as FALSE value.

Python programming language provides following types of decision making statements. Click the following links to check their detail.

Sr.No.	Statement & Description
1	**if statements** An if statement consists of a boolean expression followed by one or more statements.
2	**if...else statements** An if statement can be followed by an optional else statement, which executes when the boolean expression is FALSE.
3	**nested if statements** You can use one if or else if statement inside another if or else ifstatement(s).

Let us go through each decision making briefly —

SINGLE STATEMENT SUITES

If the suite of an if clause consists only of a single line, it may go on the same line as the header statement.

Here is an example of a one-line if clause —

```
#!/usr/bin/python

var = 100
if ( var == 100 ) : print "Value of expression is 100"
print "Good bye!"
```

When the above code is executed, it produces the following result —

```
Value of expression is 100
Good bye!
```

PYTHON - LOOPS

In general, statements are executed sequentially: The first statement in a function is executed first, followed by the second, and so on. There may be a situation when you need to execute a block of code several number of times.

Programming languages provide various control structures that allow for more complicated execution paths.

A loop statement allows us to execute a statement or group of statements multiple times. The following diagram illustrates a loop statement —

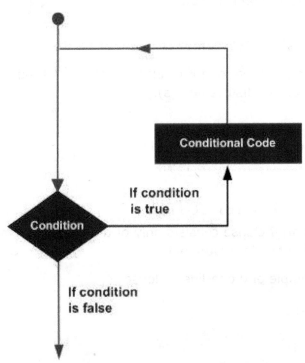

Python programming language provides following types of loops to handle looping requirements.

Sr.No.	Loop Type & Description
1	**while loop** Repeats a statement or group of statements while a given condition is TRUE. It tests the condition before executing the loop body.
2	**for loop** Executes a sequence of statements multiple times and abbreviates the code that manages the loop variable.
3	**nested loops** You can use one or more loop inside any another while, for or do..while loop.

LOOP CONTROL STATEMENTS

Loop control statements change execution from its normal sequence. When execution leaves a scope, all automatic objects that were created in that scope are destroyed.

Python supports the following control statements. Click the following links to check their detail.

Sr.No.	Control Statement & Description
1	**break statement** Terminates the loop statement and transfers execution to the statement immediately following the loop.
2	**continue statement** Causes the loop to skip the remainder of its body and immediately retest its condition prior to reiterating.
3	**pass statement** The pass statement in Python is used when a statement is required syntactically but you do not want any command or code to execute.

Let us go through the loop control statements briefly

PYTHON - NUMBERS

Number data types store numeric values. They are immutable data types, means that changing the value of a number data type results in a newly allocated object.

Number objects are created when you assign a value to them. For example −

```
var1 = 1
var2 = 10
```

You can also delete the reference to a number object by using the delstatement. The syntax of the del statement is −

```
del var1[,var2[,var3[....,varN]]]
```

You can delete a single object or multiple objects by using the del statement. For example −

```
del var
del var_a, var_b
```

Python supports four different numerical types −

- int (signed integers) − They are often called just integers or ints, are positive or negative whole numbers with no decimal point.

- long (long integers) − Also called longs, they are integers of unlimited size, written like integers and followed by an uppercase or lowercase L.

- float (floating point real values) − Also called floats, they represent real numbers and are written with a decimal point dividing the integer and fractional parts. Floats may also be in scientific notation, with E or e indicating the power of 10 (2.5e2 = 2.5 x 10^2 = 250).

- complex (complex numbers) − are of the form a + bJ, where a and b are floats and J (or j) represents the square root of -1 (which is an imaginary number). The real part of the number is a, and the imaginary part is b. Complex numbers are not used much in Python programming.

EXAMPLES

Here are some examples of numbers

int	long	float	complex
10	51924361L	0.0	3.14j
100	-0x19323L	15.20	45.j
-786	0122L	-21.9	9.322e-36j
080	0xDEFABCECBDAECBFBAEL	32.3+e18	.876j
-0490	535633629843L	-90.	-.6545+0J
-0x260	-052318172735L	-32.54e100	3e+26J
0x69	-4721885298529L	70.2-E12	4.53e-7j

- Python allows you to use a lowercase L with long, but it is recommended that you use only an uppercase L to avoid confusion with the number 1. Python displays long integers with an uppercase L.

- A complex number consists of an ordered pair of real floating point numbers denoted by a + bj, where a is the real part and b is the imaginary part of the complex number.

NUMBER TYPE CONVERSION

Python converts numbers internally in an expression containing mixed types to a common type for evaluation. But sometimes, you need to coerce a number explicitly from one type to another to satisfy the requirements of an operator or function parameter.

- Type int(x) to convert x to a plain integer.

- Type long(x) to convert x to a long integer.

- Type float(x) to convert x to a floating-point number.

- Type complex(x) to convert x to a complex number with real part x and imaginary part zero.

- Type complex(x, y) to convert x and y to a complex number with real part x and imaginary part y. x and y are numeric expressions

MATHEMATICAL FUNCTIONS

Python includes following functions that perform mathematical calculations.

Sr.No.	Function & Returns (description)
1	**abs(x)** The absolute value of x: the (positive) distance between x and zero.
2	**ceil(x)** The ceiling of x: the smallest integer not less than x
3	**cmp(x, y)** -1 if x < y, 0 if x == y, or 1 if x > y
4	**exp(x)** The exponential of x: e^x
5	**fabs(x)** The absolute value of x.
6	**floor(x)** The floor of x: the largest integer not greater than x
7	**log(x)** The natural logarithm of x, for x> 0

8   **log10(x)**

The base-10 logarithm of x for x> 0.

9   **max(x1, x2,...)**

The largest of its arguments: the value closest to positive infinity

10   **min(x1, x2,...)**

The smallest of its arguments: the value closest to negative infinity

11   **modf(x)**

The fractional and integer parts of x in a two-item tuple. Both parts have the same sign as x. The integer part is returned as a float.

12   **pow(x, y)**

The value of x**y.

13   **round(x [,n])**

x rounded to n digits from the decimal point. Python rounds away from zero as a tie-breaker: round(0.5) is 1.0 and round(-0.5) is -1.0.

14   **sqrt(x)**

The square root of x for x > 0

Random Number Functions

Random numbers are used for games, simulations, testing, security, and privacy applications. Python includes following functions that are commonly used.

Sr.No.	Function & Description
1	**choice(seq)** A random item from a list, tuple, or string.
2	**randrange ([start,] stop [,step])** A randomly selected element from range(start, stop, step)
3	**random()** A random float r, such sthat 0 is less than or equal to r and r is less than 1
4	**seed([x])** Sets the integer starting value used in generating random numbers. Call this function before calling any other random module function. Returns None.
5	**shuffle(lst)** Randomizes the items of a list in place. Returns None.
6	**uniform(x, y)** A random float r, such that x is less than or equal to r and r is less than y

TRIGONOMETRIC FUNCTIONS

Python includes following functions that perform trigonometric calculations.

Sr.No.	Function & Description
1	**acos(x)** Return the arc cosine of x, in radians.
2	**asin(x)** Return the arc sine of x, in radians.
3	**atan(x)** Return the arc tangent of x, in radians.
4	**atan2(y, x)** Return atan(y / x), in radians.
5	**cos(x)** Return the cosine of x radians.

6	**hypot(x, y)** Return the Euclidean norm, sqrt(x*x + y*y).
7	**sin(x)** Return the sine of x radians.
8	**tan(x)** Return the tangent of x radians.
9	**degrees(x)** Converts angle x from radians to degrees.
10	**radians(x)** Converts angle x from degrees to radians.

MATHEMATICAL CONSTANTS

The module also defines two mathematical constants –

Sr.No.	Constants & Description
1	pi The mathematical constant pi.
2	e The mathematical constant e.

Python - Strings

Strings are amongst the most popular types in Python. We can create them simply by enclosing characters in quotes. Python treats single quotes the same as double quotes. Creating strings is as simple as assigning a value to a variable. For example –

```
var1 = 'Hello World!'
var2 = "Python Programming"
```

Accessing Values in Strings

Python does not support a character type; these are treated as strings of length one, thus also considered a substring.

To access substrings, use the square brackets for slicing along with the index or indices to obtain your substring. For example –

```
#!/usr/bin/python

var1 = 'Hello World!'
var2 = "Python Programming"

print "var1[0]: ", var1[0]
print "var2[1:5]: ", var2[1:5]
```

When the above code is executed, it produces the following result –

```
var1[0]:  H
var2[1:5]:  ytho
```

UPDATING STRINGS

You can "update" an existing string by (re)assigning a variable to another string. The new value can be related to its previous value or to a completely different string altogether. For example —

```
#!/usr/bin/python

var1 = 'Hello World!'

print "Updated String :- ", var1[:6] + 'Python'
```

When the above code is executed, it produces the following result —

```
Updated String :-  Hello Python
```

ESCAPE CHARACTERS

Following table is a list of escape or non-printable characters that can be represented with backslash notation.

An escape character gets interpreted; in a single quoted as well as double quoted strings.

Backslash notation	Hexadecimal character	Description
\a	0x07	Bell or alert
\b	0x08	Backspace

\cx		Control-x
\C-x		Control-x
\e	0x1b	Escape
\f	0x0c	Formfeed
\M-\C-x		Meta-Control-x
\n	0x0a	Newline
\nnn		Octal notation, where n is in the range 0.7
\r	0x0d	Carriage return
\s	0x20	Space
\t	0x09	Tab
\v	0x0b	Vertical tab
\x		Character x
\xnn		Hexadecimal notation, where n is in the range 0.9, a.f, or A.F

STRING SPECIAL OPERATORS

Assume string variable a holds 'Hello' and variable b holds 'Python', then —

Operator	Description	Example
+	Concatenation - Adds values on either side of the operator	a + b will give HelloPython
*	Repetition - Creates new strings, concatenating multiple copies of the same string	a*2 will give - HelloHello
[]	Slice - Gives the character from the given index	a[1] will give e
[:]	Range Slice - Gives the characters from the given range	a[1:4] will give ell
in	Membership - Returns true if a character exists in the given string	H in a will give 1
not in	Membership - Returns true if a character does not exist in the given string	M not in a will give 1

r/R	Raw String - Suppresses actual meaning of Escape characters. The syntax for raw strings is exactly the same as for normal strings with the exception of the raw string operator, the letter "r," which precedes the quotation marks. The "r" can be lowercase (r) or uppercase (R) and must be placed immediately preceding the first quote mark.	print r'\n' prints \n and print R'\n'prints \n
%	Format - Performs String formatting	See at next section

STRING FORMATTING OPERATOR

One of Python's coolest features is the string format operator %. This operator is unique to strings and makes up for the pack of having functions from C's printf() family. Following is a simple example −

```
#!/usr/bin/python
```

```
print "My name is %s and weight is %d kg!" % ('Zara', 21)
```

When the above code is executed, it produces the following result −

```
My name is Zara and weight is 21 kg!
```

Here is the list of complete set of symbols which can be used along with % −

Format Symbol	Conversion
%c	character
%s	string conversion via str() prior to formatting
%i	signed decimal integer
%d	signed decimal integer
%u	unsigned decimal integer
%o	octal integer
%x	hexadecimal integer (lowercase letters)
%X	hexadecimal integer (UPPERcase letters)
%e	exponential notation (with lowercase 'e')
%E	exponential notation (with UPPERcase 'E')
%f	floating point real number
%g	the shorter of %f and %e

Symbol	Functionality
%G	the shorter of %f and %E

Other supported symbols and functionality are listed in the following table –

Symbol	Functionality
*	argument specifies width or precision
-	left justification
+	display the sign
<sp>	leave a blank space before a positive number
#	add the octal leading zero ('0') or hexadecimal leading '0x' or '0X', depending on whether 'x' or 'X' were used.
0	pad from left with zeros (instead of spaces)
%	'%%' leaves you with a single literal '%'
(var)	mapping variable (dictionary arguments)
m.n.	m is the minimum total width and n is the number of digits to display after the decimal point (if appl.)

Triple Quotes

Python's triple quotes comes to the rescue by allowing strings to span multiple lines, including verbatim NEWLINEs, TABs, and any other special characters.

The syntax for triple quotes consists of three consecutive single or doublequotes.

```
#!/usr/bin/python
```

```
para_str = """this is a long string that is made up of
several lines and non-printable characters such as
TAB ( \t ) and they will show up that way when displayed.
NEWLINEs within the string, whether explicitly given like
this within the brackets [ \n ], or just a NEWLINE within
the variable assignment will also show up.
"""
print para_str
```

When the above code is executed, it produces the following result. Note how every single special character has been converted to its printed form, right down to the last NEWLINE at the end of the string between the "up." and closing triple quotes. Also note that NEWLINEs occur either with an explicit carriage return at the end of a line or its escape code (\n) −

```
this is a long string that is made up of
several lines and non-printable characters such as
TAB (    ) and they will show up that way when displayed.
NEWLINEs within the string, whether explicitly given like
this within the brackets [
 ], or just a NEWLINE within
the variable assignment will also show up.
```

Raw strings do not treat the backslash as a special character at all. Every character you put into a raw string stays the way you wrote it −

```
#!/usr/bin/python
```

```
print 'C:\\nowhere'
```

When the above code is executed, it produces the following result —

```
C:\nowhere
```

Now let's make use of raw string. We would put expression in r'expression'as follows —

```
#!/usr/bin/python
```

```
print r'C:\\nowhere'
```

When the above code is executed, it produces the following result —

```
C:\\nowhere
```

UNICODE STRING

Normal strings in Python are stored internally as 8-bit ASCII, while Unicode strings are stored as 16-bit Unicode. This allows for a more varied set of characters, including special characters from most languages in the world. I'll restrict my treatment of Unicode strings to the following —

```
#!/usr/bin/python
```

```
print u'Hello, world!'
```

When the above code is executed, it produces the following result —

```
Hello, world!
```

As you can see, Unicode strings use the prefix u, just as raw strings use the prefix r.

Built-in String Methods

Python includes the following built-in methods to manipulate strings —

Sr.No.	Methods with Description
1	**capitalize()** Capitalizes first letter of string
2	**center(width, fillchar)** Returns a space-padded string with the original string centered to a total of width columns.
3	**count(str, beg= 0,end=len(string))** Counts how many times str occurs in string or in a substring of string if starting index beg and ending index end are given.
4	**decode(encoding='UTF-8',errors='strict')** Decodes the string using the codec registered for encoding. encoding defaults to the default string encoding.

5	**encode(encoding='UTF-8',errors='strict')** Returns encoded string version of string; on error, default is to raise a ValueError unless errors is given with 'ignore' or 'replace'.
6	**endswith(suffix, beg=0, end=len(string))** Determines if string or a substring of string (if starting index beg and ending index end are given) ends with suffix; returns true if so and false otherwise.
7	**expandtabs(tabsize=8)** Expands tabs in string to multiple spaces; defaults to 8 spaces per tab if tabsize not provided.
8	**find(str, beg=0 end=len(string))** Determine if str occurs in string or in a substring of string if starting index beg and ending index end are given returns index if found and -1 otherwise.
9	**index(str, beg=0, end=len(string))** Same as find(), but raises an exception if str not

found.

10   **isalnum()**

Returns true if string has at least 1 character and all characters are alphanumeric and false otherwise.

11   **isalpha()**

Returns true if string has at least 1 character and all characters are alphabetic and false otherwise.

12   **isdigit()**

Returns true if string contains only digits and false otherwise.

13   **islower()**

Returns true if string has at least 1 cased character and all cased characters are in lowercase and false otherwise.

14	**isnumeric()** Returns true if a unicode string contains only numeric characters and false otherwise.
15	**isspace()** Returns true if string contains only whitespace characters and false otherwise.
16	**istitle()** Returns true if string is properly "titlecased" and false otherwise.
17	**isupper()** Returns true if string has at least one cased character and all cased characters are in uppercase and false otherwise.
18	**join(seq)** Merges (concatenates) the string representations of elements in sequence seq into a string, with separator string.

19   **len(string)**

Returns the length of the string

20   **ljust(width[, fillchar])**

Returns a space-padded string with the original string left-justified to a total of width columns.

21   **lower()**

Converts all uppercase letters in string to lowercase.

22   **lstrip()**

Removes all leading whitespace in string.

23   **maketrans()**

Returns a translation table to be used in translate function.

24   **max(str)**

Returns the max alphabetical character from the string str.

25	**<u>min(str)</u>** Returns the min alphabetical character from the string str.
26	**<u>replace(old, new [, max])</u>** Replaces all occurrences of old in string with new or at most max occurrences if max given.
27	**<u>rfind(str, beg=0,end=len(string))</u>** Same as find(), but search backwards in string.
28	**<u>rindex(str, beg=0, end=len(string))</u>** Same as index(), but search backwards in string.
29	**<u>rjust(width,[, fillchar])</u>** Returns a space-padded string with the original string right-justified to a total of width columns.
30	**<u>rstrip()</u>** Removes all trailing whitespace of string.

31   **split(str="", num=string.count(str))**

Splits string according to delimiter str (space if not provided) and returns list of substrings; split into at most num substrings if given.

32   **splitlines(num=string.count('\n'))**

Splits string at all (or num) NEWLINEs and returns a list of each line with NEWLINEs removed.

33   **startswith(str, beg=0,end=len(string))**

Determines if string or a substring of string (if starting index beg and ending index end are given) starts with substring str; returns true if so and false otherwise.

34   **strip([chars])**

Performs both lstrip() and rstrip() on string.

35   **swapcase()**

Inverts case for all letters in string.

36	**title()**
	Returns "titlecased" version of string, that is, all words begin with uppercase and the rest are lowercase.

37	**translate(table, deletechars="")**
	Translates string according to translation table str(256 chars), removing those in the del string.

38	**upper()**
	Converts lowercase letters in string to uppercase.

39	**zfill (width)**
	Returns original string leftpadded with zeros to a total of width characters; intended for numbers, zfill() retains any sign given (less one zero).

40	**isdecimal()**
	Returns true if a unicode string contains only decimal characters and false otherwise.

PYTHON - LISTS

The most basic data structure in Python is the sequence. Each element of a sequence is assigned a number - its position or index. The first index is zero, the second index is one, and so forth.

Python has six built-in types of sequences, but the most common ones are lists and tuples, which we would see in this tutorial.

There are certain things you can do with all sequence types. These operations include indexing, slicing, adding, multiplying, and checking for membership. In addition, Python has built-in functions for finding the length of a sequence and for finding its largest and smallest elements.

PYTHON LISTS

The list is a most versatile datatype available in Python which can be written as a list of comma-separated values (items) between square brackets. Important thing about a list is that items in a list need not be of the same type.

Creating a list is as simple as putting different comma-separated values between square brackets. For example −

```
list1 = ['physics', 'chemistry', 1997, 2000];
list2 = [1, 2, 3, 4, 5 ];
list3 = ["a", "b", "c", "d"]
```

Similar to string indices, list indices start at 0, and lists can be sliced, concatenated and so on.

ACCESSING VALUES IN LISTS

To access values in lists, use the square brackets for slicing along with the index or indices to obtain value available at that index. For example —

```
#!/usr/bin/python

list1 = ['physics', 'chemistry', 1997, 2000];
list2 = [1, 2, 3, 4, 5, 6, 7 ];

print "list1[0]: ", list1[0]
print "list2[1:5]: ", list2[1:5]
```

When the above code is executed, it produces the following result —

```
list1[0]:  physics
list2[1:5]:  [2, 3, 4, 5]
```

UPDATING LISTS

You can update single or multiple elements of lists by giving the slice on the left-hand side of the assignment operator, and you can add to elements in a list with the append() method. For example —

```
#!/usr/bin/python

list = ['physics', 'chemistry', 1997, 2000];

print "Value available at index 2 : "
print list[2]
list[2] = 2001;
print "New value available at index 2 : "
print list[2]
```

Note — append() method is discussed in subsequent section.

When the above code is executed, it produces the following result —

```
Value available at index 2 :
1997
New value available at index 2 :
2001
```

DELETE LIST ELEMENTS

To remove a list element, you can use either the del statement if you know exactly which element(s) you are deleting or the remove() method if you do not know. For example —

```
#!/usr/bin/python

list1 = ['physics', 'chemistry', 1997, 2000];

print list1
del list1[2];
print "After deleting value at index 2 : "
print list1
```

When the above code is executed, it produces following result —

```
['physics', 'chemistry', 1997, 2000]
After deleting value at index 2 :
['physics', 'chemistry', 2000]
```

Note — remove() method is discussed in subsequent section.

Basic List Operations

Lists respond to the + and * operators much like strings; they mean concatenation and repetition here too, except that the result is a new list, not a string.

In fact, lists respond to all of the general sequence operations we used on strings in the prior chapter.

Python Expression	Results	Description
len([1, 2, 3])	3	Length
[1, 2, 3] + [4, 5, 6]	[1, 2, 3, 4, 5, 6]	Concatenation
['Hi!'] * 4	['Hi!', 'Hi!', 'Hi!', 'Hi!']	Repetition
3 in [1, 2, 3]	True	Membership
for x in [1, 2, 3]: print x,	1 2 3	Iteration

INDEXING, SLICING, AND MATRIXES

Because lists are sequences, indexing and slicing work the same way for lists as they do for strings.

Assuming following input –

```
L = ['spam', 'Spam', 'SPAM!']
```

Python Expression	Results	Description
L[2]	'SPAM!'	Offsets start at zero
L[-2]	'Spam'	Negative: count from the right
L[1:]	['Spam', 'SPAM!']	Slicing fetches sections

BUILT-IN LIST FUNCTIONS & METHODS

Python includes the following list functions –

Sr.No.	Function with Description
1	cmp(list1, list2) Compares elements of both lists.

2	len(list) Gives the total length of the list.
3	max(list) Returns item from the list with max value.
4	min(list) Returns item from the list with min value.
5	list(seq) Converts a tuple into list.

Python includes following list methods

Sr.No.	Methods with Description
1	list.append(obj) Appends object obj to list
2	list.count(obj) Returns count of how many times obj occurs in list

3   list.extend(seq)

         Appends the contents of seq to list

4   list.index(obj)

         Returns the lowest index in list that obj appears

5   list.insert(index, obj)

         Inserts object obj into list at offset index

6   list.pop(obj=list[-1])

         Removes and returns last object or obj from list

7   list.remove(obj)

         Removes object obj from list

8   list.reverse()

         Reverses objects of list in place

9   list.sort([func])

         Sorts objects of list, use compare func if given

PYTHON - TUPLES

A tuple is a sequence of immutable Python objects. Tuples are sequences, just like lists. The differences between tuples and lists are, the tuples cannot be changed unlike lists and tuples use parentheses, whereas lists use square brackets.

Creating a tuple is as simple as putting different comma-separated values. Optionally you can put these comma-separated values between parentheses also. For example –

```
tup1 = ('physics', 'chemistry', 1997, 2000);
tup2 = (1, 2, 3, 4, 5 );
tup3 = "a", "b", "c", "d";
```

The empty tuple is written as two parentheses containing nothing –

```
tup1 = ();
```

To write a tuple containing a single value you have to include a comma, even though there is only one value –

```
tup1 = (50,);
```

Like string indices, tuple indices start at 0, and they can be sliced, concatenated, and so on.

ACCESSING VALUES IN TUPLES

To access values in tuple, use the square brackets for slicing along with the index or indices to obtain value available at that index. For example —

```
#!/usr/bin/python

tup1 = ('physics', 'chemistry', 1997, 2000);
tup2 = (1, 2, 3, 4, 5, 6, 7 );

print "tup1[0]: ", tup1[0];
print "tup2[1:5]: ", tup2[1:5];
```

When the above code is executed, it produces the following result —

```
tup1[0]:  physics
tup2[1:5]:  (2, 3, 4, 5)
```

UPDATING TUPLES

Tuples are immutable which means you cannot update or change the values of tuple elements. You are able to take portions of existing tuples to create new tuples as the following example demonstrates —

```
#!/usr/bin/python
tup1 = (12, 34.56);
tup2 = ('abc', 'xyz');

# Following action is not valid for tuples
# tup1[0] = 100;
# So let's create a new tuple as follows
tup3 = tup1 + tup2;
print tup3;
```

When the above code is executed, it produces the following result —

```
(12, 34.56, 'abc', 'xyz')
```

DELETE TUPLE ELEMENTS

Removing individual tuple elements is not possible. There is, of course, nothing wrong with putting together another tuple with the undesired elements discarded.

To explicitly remove an entire tuple, just use the del statement. For example −

```
#!/usr/bin/python

tup = ('physics', 'chemistry', 1997, 2000);

print tup;
del tup;
print "After deleting tup : ";
print tup;
```

This produces the following result. Note an exception raised, this is because after del tup tuple does not exist any more −

```
('physics', 'chemistry', 1997, 2000)
After deleting tup :
Traceback (most recent call last):
   File "test.py", line 9, in <module>
       print tup;
NameError: name 'tup' is not defined
```

BASIC TUPLES OPERATIONS

Tuples respond to the + and * operators much like strings; they mean concatenation and repetition here too, except that the result is a new tuple, not a string.

In fact, tuples respond to all of the general sequence operations we used on strings in the prior chapter –

Python Expression	Results	Description
len((1, 2, 3))	3	Length
(1, 2, 3) + (4, 5, 6)	(1, 2, 3, 4, 5, 6)	Concatenation
('Hi!',) * 4	('Hi!', 'Hi!', 'Hi!', 'Hi!')	Repetition
3 in (1, 2, 3)	True	Membership
for x in (1, 2, 3): print x,	1 2 3	Iteration

INDEXING, SLICING, AND MATRIXES

Because tuples are sequences, indexing and slicing work the same way for tuples as they do for strings. Assuming following input –

```
L = ('spam', 'Spam', 'SPAM!')
```

Python Expression	Results	Description
L[2]	'SPAM!'	Offsets start at zero
L[-2]	'Spam'	Negative: count from the right
L[1:]	['Spam', 'SPAM!']	Slicing fetches sections

NO ENCLOSING DELIMITERS

Any set of multiple objects, comma-separated, written without identifying symbols, i.e., brackets for lists, parentheses for tuples, etc., default to tuples, as indicated in these short examples –

```
#!/usr/bin/python

print 'abc', -4.24e93, 18+6.6j, 'xyz';
x, y = 1, 2;
print "Value of x , y : ", x,y;
```

When the above code is executed, it produces the following result –

```
abc -4.24e+93 (18+6.6j) xyz
Value of x , y : 1 2
```

BUILT-IN TUPLE FUNCTIONS

Python includes the following tuple functions –

Sr.No.	Function with Description
1	**cmp(tuple1, tuple2)** Compares elements of both tuples.
2	**len(tuple)** Gives the total length of the tuple.
3	**max(tuple)** Returns item from the tuple with max value.
4	**min(tuple)** Returns item from the tuple with min value.
5	**tuple(seq)** Converts a list into tuple.

Python - Dictionary

Each key is separated from its value by a colon (:), the items are separated by commas, and the whole thing is enclosed in curly braces. An empty dictionary without any items is written with just two curly braces, like this: {}.

Keys are unique within a dictionary while values may not be. The values of a dictionary can be of any type, but the keys must be of an immutable data type such as strings, numbers, or tuples.

Accessing Values in Dictionary

To access dictionary elements, you can use the familiar square brackets along with the key to obtain its value. Following is a simple example —

```
#!/usr/bin/python

dict = {'Name': 'Zara', 'Age': 7, 'Class': 'First'}

print "dict['Name']: ", dict['Name']
print "dict['Age']: ", dict['Age']
```

When the above code is executed, it produces the following result —

```
dict['Name']:  Zara
dict['Age']:  7
```

If we attempt to access a data item with a key, which is not part of the dictionary, we get an error as follows —

```
#!/usr/bin/python

dict = {'Name': 'Zara', 'Age': 7, 'Class': 'First'}

print "dict['Alice']: ", dict['Alice']
```

When the above code is executed, it produces the following result −

```
dict['Alice']:
Traceback (most recent call last):
   File "test.py", line 4, in <module>
      print "dict['Alice']: ", dict['Alice'];
KeyError: 'Alice'
```

UPDATING DICTIONARY

You can update a dictionary by adding a new entry or a key-value pair, modifying an existing entry, or deleting an existing entry as shown below in the simple example −

```
#!/usr/bin/python

dict = {'Name': 'Zara', 'Age': 7, 'Class': 'First'}

dict['Age'] = 8; # update existing entry
dict['School'] = "DPS School"; # Add new entry


print "dict['Age']: ", dict['Age']
print "dict['School']: ", dict['School']
```

When the above code is executed, it produces the following result −

```
dict['Age']:  8
dict['School']:  DPS School
```

DELETE DICTIONARY ELEMENTS

You can either remove individual dictionary elements or clear the entire contents of a dictionary. You can also delete entire dictionary in a single operation.

To explicitly remove an entire dictionary, just use the del statement. Following is a simple example −

```
#!/usr/bin/python

dict = {'Name': 'Zara', 'Age': 7, 'Class': 'First'}

del dict['Name']; # remove entry with key 'Name'
dict.clear();      # remove all entries in dict
del dict ;         # delete entire dictionary

print "dict['Age']: ", dict['Age']
print "dict['School']: ", dict['School']
```

This produces the following result. Note that an exception is raised because after del dict dictionary does not exist any more −

```
dict['Age']:
Traceback (most recent call last):
   File "test.py", line 8, in <module>
      print "dict['Age']: ", dict['Age'];
TypeError: 'type' object is unsubscriptable
```

Note − del() method is discussed in subsequent section.

PROPERTIES OF DICTIONARY KEYS

Dictionary values have no restrictions. They can be any arbitrary Python object, either standard objects or user-defined objects. However, same is not true for the keys.

There are two important points to remember about dictionary keys −

(a) More than one entry per key not allowed. Which means no duplicate key is allowed. When duplicate keys encountered during assignment, the last assignment wins. For example −

```
#!/usr/bin/python

dict = {'Name': 'Zara', 'Age': 7, 'Name': 'Manni'}

print "dict['Name']: ", dict['Name']
```

When the above code is executed, it produces the following result -

```
dict['Name']:  Manni
```

(b) Keys must be immutable. Which means you can use strings, numbers or tuples as dictionary keys but something like ['key'] is not allowed. Following is a simple example —

```
#!/usr/bin/python

dict = {['Name']: 'Zara', 'Age': 7}

print "dict['Name']: ", dict['Name']
```

When the above code is executed, it produces the following result —

```
Traceback (most recent call last):
    File "test.py", line 3, in <module>
        dict = {['Name']: 'Zara', 'Age': 7};
TypeError: list objects are unhashable
```

BUILT-IN DICTIONARY FUNCTIONS & METHODS

Python includes the following dictionary functions —

Sr.No.	Function with Description
1	**cmp(dict1, dict2)** Compares elements of both dict.
2	**len(dict)** Gives the total length of the dictionary. This would be equal to the number of items in the dictionary.
3	**str(dict)** Produces a printable string representation of a dictionary
4	**type(variable)** Returns the type of the passed variable. If passed variable is dictionary, then it would return a dictionary type.

Python includes following dictionary methods —

1   **dict.clear()**

Removes all elements of dictionary *dict*

2   **dict.copy()**

Returns a shallow copy of dictionary *dict*

3   **dict.fromkeys()**

Create a new dictionary with keys from seq and values *set* to *value*.

4   **dict.get(key, default=None)**

For *key* key, returns value or default if key not in dictionary

5   **dict.has_key(key)**

Returns *true* if key in dictionary *dict*, *false* otherwise

6   **dict.items()**

Returns a list of *dict*'s (key, value) tuple pairs

7   **dict.keys()**

Returns list of dictionary dict's keys

8	**dict.setdefault(key, default=None)** Similar to get(), but will set dict[key]=default if *key* is not already in dict
9	**dict.update(dict2)** Adds dictionary *dict2*'s key-values pairs to *dict*
10	**dict.values()** Returns list of dictionary *dict*'s values

Python - Date & Time

A Python program can handle date and time in several ways. Converting between date formats is a common chore for computers. Python's time and calendar modules help track dates and times.

What is Tick?

Time intervals are floating-point numbers in units of seconds. Particular instants in time are expressed in seconds since 12:00am, January 1, 1970(epoch).

There is a popular time module available in Python which provides functions for working with times, and for converting between representations. The function *time.time()* returns the current system time in ticks since 12:00am, January 1, 1970(epoch).

Example

```
#!/usr/bin/python
import time;  # This is required to include time module.

ticks = time.time()
print "Number of ticks since 12:00am, January 1, 1970:", ticks
```

This would produce a result something as follows −

```
Number of ticks since 12:00am, January 1, 1970: 7186862.73399
```

Date arithmetic is easy to do with ticks. However, dates before the epoch cannot be represented in this form. Dates in the far future also cannot be represented this way - the cutoff point is sometime in 2038 for UNIX and Windows.

WHAT IS TIMETUPLE?

Many of Python's time functions handle time as a tuple of 9 numbers, as shown below –

Index	Field	Values
0	4-digit year	2008
1	Month	1 to 12
2	Day	1 to 31
3	Hour	0 to 23
4	Minute	0 to 59
5	Second	0 to 61 (60 or 61 are leap-seconds)
6	Day of Week	0 to 6 (0 is Monday)
7	Day of year	1 to 366 (Julian day)
8	Daylight savings	-1, 0, 1, -1 means library determines DST

The above tuple is equivalent to struct_time structure. This structure has following attributes –

Index	Attributes	Values
0	tm_year	2008
1	tm_mon	1 to 12
2	tm_mday	1 to 31
3	tm_hour	0 to 23
4	tm_min	0 to 59
5	tm_sec	0 to 61 (60 or 61 are leap-seconds)
6	tm_wday	0 to 6 (0 is Monday)
7	tm_yday	1 to 366 (Julian day)
8	tm_isdst	-1, 0, 1, -1 means library determines DST

GETTING CURRENT TIME

To translate a time instant from a *seconds since the epoch* floating-point value into a time-tuple, pass the floating-point value to a function (e.g., localtime) that returns a time-tuple with all nine items valid.

```
#!/usr/bin/python
import time;

localtime = time.localtime(time.time())
print "Local current time :", localtime
```

This would produce the following result, which could be formatted in any other presentable form —

```
Local current time : time.struct_time(tm_year=2013, tm_mon=7,
tm_mday=17, tm_hour=21, tm_min=26, tm_sec=3, tm_wday=2, tm_yday=198,
tm_isdst=0)
```

GETTING FORMATTED TIME

You can format any time as per your requirement, but simple method to get time in readable format is asctime() —

```
#!/usr/bin/python
import time;

localtime = time.asctime( time.localtime(time.time()) )
print "Local current time :", localtime
```

This would produce the following result —

```
Local current time : Tue Jan 13 10:17:09 2009
```

GETTING CALENDAR FOR A MONTH

The calendar module gives a wide range of methods to play with yearly and monthly calendars. Here, we print a calendar for a given month (Jan 2008) –

```
#!/usr/bin/python
import calendar

cal = calendar.month(2008, 1)
print "Here is the calendar:"
print cal
```

This would produce the following result –

```
Here is the calendar:
    January 2008
Mo Tu We Th Fr Sa Su
    1  2  3  4  5  6
 7  8  9 10 11 12 13
14 15 16 17 18 19 20
21 22 23 24 25 26 27
28 29 30 31
```

THE *TIME* MODULE

There is a popular time module available in Python which provides functions for working with times and for converting between representations. Here is the list of all available methods –

Sr.No.	Function with Description
1	**time.altzone** The offset of the local DST timezone, in seconds west of UTC, if one is defined. This is negative if the local DST timezone is east of UTC (as in Western Europe, including the UK). Only use this if daylight is nonzero.
2	**time.asctime([tupletime])** Accepts a time-tuple and returns a readable 24-character string such as 'Tue Dec 11 18:07:14 2008'.
3	**time.clock( )** Returns the current CPU time as a floating-point number of seconds. To measure computational costs of different approaches, the value of time.clock is more useful than that of time.time().
4	**time.ctime([secs])** Like asctime(localtime(secs)) and without arguments is like asctime( )

5   **time.gmtime([secs])**

Accepts an instant expressed in seconds since the epoch and returns a time-tuple t with the UTC time. Note : t.tm_isdst is always 0

6   **time.localtime([secs])**

Accepts an instant expressed in seconds since the epoch and returns a time-tuple t with the local time (t.tm_isdst is 0 or 1, depending on whether DST applies to instant secs by local rules).

7   **time.mktime(tupletime)**

Accepts an instant expressed as a time-tuple in local time and returns a floating-point value with the instant expressed in seconds since the epoch.

8   **time.sleep(secs)**

Suspends the calling thread for secs seconds.

9   **time.strftime(fmt[,tupletime])**

Accepts an instant expressed as a time-tuple in local time and returns a string representing the instant as specified by string fmt.

10   **time.strptime(str,fmt='%a   %b   %d %H:%M:%S %Y')**

Parses str according to format string fmt and returns the instant in time-tuple format.

11	**time.time( )**
	Returns the current time instant, a floating-point number of seconds since the epoch.
12	**time.tzset()**
	Resets the time conversion rules used by the library routines. The environment variable TZ specifies how this is done.

Let us go through the functions briefly —

There are following two important attributes available with time module —

Sr.No.	Attribute with Description
1	time.timezone
	Attribute time.timezone is the offset in seconds of the local time zone (without DST) from UTC (>0 in the Americas; <=0 in most of Europe, Asia, Africa).
2	time.tzname
	Attribute time.tzname is a pair of locale-dependent strings, which are the names of the local time zone without and with DST, respectively.

THE *CALENDAR* MODULE

The calendar module supplies calendar-related functions, including functions to print a text calendar for a given month or year.

By default, calendar takes Monday as the first day of the week and Sunday as the last one. To change this, call calendar.setfirstweekday() function.

Here is a list of functions available with the calendar module –

Sr.No.	Function with Description
1	calendar.calendar(year,w=2,l=1,c=6) Returns a multiline string with a calendar for year year formatted into three columns separated by c spaces. w is the width in characters of each date; each line has length 21*w+18+2*c. l is the number of lines for each week.
2	calendar.firstweekday( ) Returns the current setting for the weekday that starts each week. By default, when calendar is first imported, this is 0, meaning Monday.
3	calendar.isleap(year) Returns True if year is a leap year; otherwise, False.

4	calendar.leapdays(y1,y2)
	Returns the total number of leap days in the years within range(y1,y2).
5	calendar.month(year,month,w=2,l=1)
	Returns a multiline string with a calendar for month month of year year, one line per week plus two header lines. w is the width in characters of each date; each line has length 7*w+6. l is the number of lines for each week.
6	calendar.monthcalendar(year,month)
	Returns a list of lists of ints. Each sublist denotes a week. Days outside month month of year year are set to 0; days within the month are set to their day-of-month, 1 and up.
7	calendar.monthrange(year,month)
	Returns two integers. The first one is the code of the weekday for the first day of the month month in year year; the second one is the number of days in the month. Weekday codes are 0 (Monday) to 6 (Sunday); month numbers are 1 to 12.

8	calendar.prcal(year,w=2,l=1,c=6)
	Like print calendar.calendar(year,w,l,c).

9	calendar.prmonth(year,month,w=2,l=1)
	Like print calendar.month(year,month,w,l).

10	calendar.setfirstweekday(weekday)
	Sets the first day of each week to weekday code weekday. Weekday codes are 0 (Monday) to 6 (Sunday).

11	calendar.timegm(tupletime)
	The inverse of time.gmtime: accepts a time instant in time-tuple form and returns the same instant as a floating-point number of seconds since the epoch.

12	calendar.weekday(year,month,day)
	Returns the weekday code for the given date. Weekday codes are 0 (Monday) to 6 (Sunday); month numbers are 1 (January) to 12 (December).

Other Modules & Functions

If you are interested, then here you would find a list of other important modules and functions to play with date & time in Python –

- The *datetime* Module
- The *pytz* Module
- The *dateutil* Module

Python - Functions

A function is a block of organized, reusable code that is used to perform a single, related action. Functions provide better modularity for your application and a high degree of code reusing.

As you already know, Python gives you many built-in functions like print(), etc. but you can also create your own functions. These functions are called *user-defined* functions.

Defining a Function

You can define functions to provide the required functionality. Here are simple rules to define a function in Python.

- Function blocks begin with the keyword def followed by the function name and parentheses (( )).

- Any input parameters or arguments should be placed within these parentheses. You can also define parameters inside these parentheses.

- The first statement of a function can be an optional statement - the documentation string of the function or *docstring*.

- The code block within every function starts with a colon (:) and is indented.

- The statement return [expression] exits a function, optionally passing back an expression to the caller. A return statement with no arguments is the same as return None.

Syntax

```
def functionname( parameters ):
    "function_docstring"
    function_suite
    return [expression]
```

By default, parameters have a positional behavior and you need to inform them in the same order that they were defined.

Example

The following function takes a string as input parameter and prints it on standard screen.

```
def printme( str ):
    "This prints a passed string into this function"
    print str
    return
```

Calling a Function

Defining a function only gives it a name, specifies the parameters that are to be included in the function and structures the blocks of code.

Once the basic structure of a function is finalized, you can execute it by calling it from another function or directly from the Python prompt. Following is the example to call printme() function —

```
#!/usr/bin/python

# Function definition is here
def printme( str ):
    "This prints a passed string into this function"
    print str
```

```
    return;
```

```
# Now you can call printme function
printme("I'm first call to user defined function!")
printme("Again second call to the same function")
```

When the above code is executed, it produces the following result —

```
I'm first call to user defined function!
Again second call to the same function
```

PASS BY REFERENCE VS VALUE

All parameters (arguments) in the Python language are passed by reference. It means if you change what a parameter refers to within a function, the change also reflects back in the calling function. For example —

```
#!/usr/bin/python
```

```
# Function definition is here
def changeme( mylist ):
    "This changes a passed list into this function"
    mylist.append([1,2,3,4]);
    print "Values inside the function: ", mylist
    return
```

```
# Now you can call changeme function
mylist = [10,20,30];
changeme( mylist );
print "Values outside the function: ", mylist
```

Here, we are maintaining reference of the passed object and appending values in the same object. So, this would produce the following result —

```
Values inside the function:   [10, 20, 30, [1, 2, 3, 4]]
Values outside the function:   [10, 20, 30, [1, 2, 3, 4]]
```

There is one more example where argument is being passed by reference and the reference is being overwritten inside the called function.

```
#!/usr/bin/python

# Function definition is here
def changeme( mylist ):
    "This changes a passed list into this function"
    mylist = [1,2,3,4]; # This would assig new reference in mylist
    print "Values inside the function: ", mylist
    return

# Now you can call changeme function
mylist = [10,20,30];
changeme( mylist );
print "Values outside the function: ", mylist
```

The parameter *mylist* is local to the function changeme. Changing mylist within the function does not affect *mylist*. The function accomplishes nothing and finally this would produce the following result −

```
Values inside the function:  [1, 2, 3, 4]
Values outside the function:  [10, 20, 30]
```

FUNCTION ARGUMENTS

You can call a function by using the following types of formal arguments −

- Required arguments
- Keyword arguments
- Default arguments
- Variable-length arguments

REQUIRED ARGUMENTS

Required arguments are the arguments passed to a function in correct positional order. Here, the number of arguments in the function call should match exactly with the function definition.

To call the function *printme()*, you definitely need to pass one argument, otherwise it gives a syntax error as follows −

```
#!/usr/bin/python

# Function definition is here
def printme( str ):
    "This prints a passed string into this function"
    print str
    return;

# Now you can call printme function
printme()
```

When the above code is executed, it produces the following result −

```
Traceback (most recent call last):
   File "test.py", line 11, in <module>
      printme();
TypeError: printme() takes exactly 1 argument (0 given)
```

KEYWORD ARGUMENTS

Keyword arguments are related to the function calls. When you use keyword arguments in a function call, the caller identifies the arguments by the parameter name.

This allows you to skip arguments or place them out of order because the Python interpreter is able to use the keywords provided to match the values with parameters. You can also make keyword calls to the *printme()* function in the following ways −

```
#!/usr/bin/python

# Function definition is here
def printme( str ):
    "This prints a passed string into this function"
    print str
    return;

# Now you can call printme function
printme( str = "My string")
```

When the above code is executed, it produces the following result –

```
My string
```

The following example gives more clear picture. Note that the order of parameters does not matter.

```
#!/usr/bin/python

# Function definition is here
def printinfo( name, age ):
    "This prints a passed info into this function"
    print "Name: ", name
    print "Age ", age
    return;

# Now you can call printinfo function
printinfo( age=50, name="miki" )
```

When the above code is executed, it produces the following result –

```
Name:  miki
Age  50
```

DEFAULT ARGUMENTS

A default argument is an argument that assumes a default value if a value is not provided in the function call for that argument. The following example gives an idea on default arguments, it prints default age if it is not passed –

```python
#!/usr/bin/python

# Function definition is here
def printinfo( name, age = 35 ):
   "This prints a passed info into this function"
   print "Name: ", name
   print "Age ", age
   return;

# Now you can call printinfo function
printinfo( age=50, name="miki" )
printinfo( name="miki" )
```

When the above code is executed, it produces the following result –

```
Name:  miki
Age  50
Name:  miki
Age  35
```

VARIABLE-LENGTH ARGUMENTS

You may need to process a function for more arguments than you specified while defining the function. These arguments are called *variable-length*arguments and are not named in the function definition, unlike required and default arguments.

Syntax for a function with non-keyword variable arguments is this –

```python
def functionname([formal_args,] *var_args_tuple ):
   "function_docstring"
   function_suite
   return [expression]
```

An asterisk (*) is placed before the variable name that holds the values of all nonkeyword variable arguments. This tuple remains empty if no additional arguments are specified during the function call. Following is a simple example −

```
#!/usr/bin/python

# Function definition is here
def printinfo( arg1, *vartuple ):
   "This prints a variable passed arguments"
   print "Output is: "
   print arg1
   for var in vartuple:
      print var
   return;

# Now you can call printinfo function
printinfo( 10 )
printinfo( 70, 60, 50 )
```

When the above code is executed, it produces the following result −

```
Output is:
10
Output is:
70
60
50
```

THE *ANONYMOUS* FUNCTIONS

These functions are called anonymous because they are not declared in the standard manner by using the *def* keyword. You can use the *lambda* keyword to create small anonymous functions.

- Lambda forms can take any number of arguments but return just one value in the form of an expression. They cannot contain commands or multiple expressions.

- An anonymous function cannot be a direct call to print because lambda requires an expression

- Lambda functions have their own local namespace and cannot access variables other than those in their parameter list and those in the global namespace.

- Although it appears that lambda's are a one-line version of a function, they are not equivalent to inline statements in C or C++, whose purpose is by passing function stack allocation during invocation for performance reasons.

SYNTAX

The syntax of *lambda* functions contains only a single statement, which is as follows −

```
lambda [arg1 [,arg2,.....argn]]:expression
```

Following is the example to show how *lambda* form of function works −

```
#!/usr/bin/python

# Function definition is here
sum = lambda arg1, arg2: arg1 + arg2;

# Now you can call sum as a function
print "Value of total : ", sum( 10, 20 )
print "Value of total : ", sum( 20, 20 )
```

When the above code is executed, it produces the following result −

```
Value of total :   30
Value of total :   40
```

THE *RETURN* STATEMENT

The statement return [expression] exits a function, optionally passing back an expression to the caller. A return statement with no arguments is the same as return None.

All the above examples are not returning any value. You can return a value from a function as follows −

```
#!/usr/bin/python

# Function definition is here
def sum( arg1, arg2 ):
    # Add both the parameters and return them."
    total = arg1 + arg2
    print "Inside the function : ", total
    return total;

# Now you can call sum function
total = sum( 10, 20 );
print "Outside the function : ", total
```

When the above code is executed, it produces the following result −

```
Inside the function :  30
Outside the function :  30
```

SCOPE OF VARIABLES

All variables in a program may not be accessible at all locations in that program. This depends on where you have declared a variable.

The scope of a variable determines the portion of the program where you can access a particular identifier. There are two basic scopes of variables in Python −

- Global variables
- Local variables

118

GLOBAL VS. LOCAL VARIABLES

Variables that are defined inside a function body have a local scope, and those defined outside have a global scope.

This means that local variables can be accessed only inside the function in which they are declared, whereas global variables can be accessed throughout the program body by all functions. When you call a function, the variables declared inside it are brought into scope. Following is a simple example –

```
#!/usr/bin/python

total = 0; # This is global variable.
# Function definition is here
def sum( arg1, arg2 ):
   # Add both the parameters and return them."
   total = arg1 + arg2; # Here total is local variable.
   print "Inside the function local total : ", total
   return total;

# Now you can call sum function
sum( 10, 20 );
print "Outside the function global total : ", total
```

When the above code is executed, it produces the following result –

```
Inside the function local total :  30
Outside the function global total :  0
```

Python - Modules

A module allows you to logically organize your Python code. Grouping related code into a module makes the code easier to understand and use. A module is a Python object with arbitrarily named attributes that you can bind and reference.

Simply, a module is a file consisting of Python code. A module can define functions, classes and variables. A module can also include runnable code.

Example

The Python code for a module named *aname* normally resides in a file named *aname.py*. Here's an example of a simple module, support.py

```python
def print_func( par ):
    print "Hello : ", par
    return
```

The *IMPORT* Statement

You can use any Python source file as a module by executing an import statement in some other Python source file. The *import* has the following syntax −

```python
import module1[, module2[,... moduleN]
```

When the interpreter encounters an import statement, it imports the module if the module is present in the search path. A search path is a list of directories that the interpreter searches before importing a module. For example, to import the module support.py, you need to put the following command at the top of the script −

```
#!/usr/bin/python

# Import module support
import support

# Now you can call defined function that module as follows
support.print_func("Zara")
```

When the above code is executed, it produces the following result —

```
Hello : Zara
```

A module is loaded only once, regardless of the number of times it is imported. This prevents the module execution from happening over and over again if multiple imports occur.

THE *FROM...IMPORT* STATEMENT

Python's *from* statement lets you import specific attributes from a module into the current namespace. The *from...import* has the following syntax —

```
from modname import name1[, name2[, ... nameN]]
```

For example, to import the function fibonacci from the module fib, use the following statement —

```
from fib import fibonacci
```

This statement does not import the entire module fib into the current namespace; it just introduces the item fibonacci from the module fib into the global symbol table of the importing module.

The from...import * Statement

It is also possible to import all names from a module into the current namespace by using the following import statement –

```
from modname import *
```

This provides an easy way to import all the items from a module into the current namespace; however, this statement should be used sparingly.

Locating Modules

When you import a module, the Python interpreter searches for the module in the following sequences –

- The current directory.
- If the module isn't found, Python then searches each directory in the shell variable PYTHONPATH.
- If all else fails, Python checks the default path. On UNIX, this default path is normally /usr/local/lib/python/.

The module search path is stored in the system module sys as the sys.pathvariable. The sys.path variable contains the current directory, PYTHONPATH, and the installation-dependent default.

The *PYTHONPATH* Variable

The PYTHONPATH is an environment variable, consisting of a list of directories. The syntax of PYTHONPATH is the same as that of the shell variable PATH.

Here is a typical PYTHONPATH from a Windows system —

```
set PYTHONPATH = c:\python20\lib;
```

And here is a typical PYTHONPATH from a UNIX system —

```
set PYTHONPATH = /usr/local/lib/python
```

Namespaces and Scoping

Variables are names (identifiers) that map to objects. A *namespace* is a dictionary of variable names (keys) and their corresponding objects (values).

A Python statement can access variables in a *local namespace* and in the *global namespace*. If a local and a global variable have the same name, the local variable shadows the global variable.

Each function has its own local namespace. Class methods follow the same scoping rule as ordinary functions.

Python makes educated guesses on whether variables are local or global. It assumes that any variable assigned a value in a function is local.

Therefore, in order to assign a value to a global variable within a function, you must first use the global statement.

The statement *global VarName* tells Python that VarName is a global variable. Python stops searching the local namespace for the variable.

For example, we define a variable *Money* in the global namespace. Within the function *Money*, we assign *Money* a value, therefore Python assumes *Money*as a local variable. However, we accessed the value of the local

123

variable *Money* before setting it, so an UnboundLocalError is the result. Uncommenting the global statement fixes the problem.

```
#!/usr/bin/python

Money = 2000
def AddMoney():
    # Uncomment the following line to fix the code:
    # global Money
    Money = Money + 1

print Money
AddMoney()
print Money
```

THE DIR( ) FUNCTION

The dir() built-in function returns a sorted list of strings containing the names defined by a module.

The list contains the names of all the modules, variables and functions that are defined in a module. Following is a simple example –

```
#!/usr/bin/python

# Import built-in module math
import math

content = dir(math)
print content
```

When the above code is executed, it produces the following result –

```
['__doc__', '__file__', '__name__', 'acos', 'asin', 'atan',
'atan2', 'ceil', 'cos', 'cosh', 'degrees', 'e', 'exp',
'fabs', 'floor', 'fmod', 'frexp', 'hypot', 'ldexp', 'log',
'log10', 'modf', 'pi', 'pow', 'radians', 'sin', 'sinh',
'sqrt', 'tan', 'tanh']
```

Here, the special string variable __*name*__ is the module's name, and __file__is the filename from which the module was loaded.

THE *GLOBALS()* AND *LOCALS()* FUNCTIONS

The *globals()* and *locals()* functions can be used to return the names in the global and local namespaces depending on the location from where they are called.

If locals() is called from within a function, it will return all the names that can be accessed locally from that function.

If globals() is called from within a function, it will return all the names that can be accessed globally from that function.

The return type of both these functions is dictionary. Therefore, names can be extracted using the keys() function.

THE *RELOAD()* FUNCTION

When the module is imported into a script, the code in the top-level portion of a module is executed only once.

Therefore, if you want to reexecute the top-level code in a module, you can use the *reload()* function. The reload() function imports a previously imported module again. The syntax of the reload() function is this –

```
reload(module_name)
```

Here, *module_name* is the name of the module you want to reload and not the string containing the module name. For example, to reload *hello* module, do the following –

```
reload(hello)
```

PACKAGES IN PYTHON

A package is a hierarchical file directory structure that defines a single Python application environment that consists of modules and subpackages and sub-subpackages, and so on.

Consider a file *Pots.py* available in *Phone* directory. This file has following line of source code −

```
#!/usr/bin/python
```

```
def Pots():
    print "I'm Pots Phone"
```

Similar way, we have another two files having different functions with the same name as above −

- *Phone/Isdn.py* file having function Isdn()
- *Phone/G3.py* file having function G3()

Now, create one more file __init__.py in *Phone* directory −

- Phone/__init__.py

To make all of your functions available when you've imported Phone, you need to put explicit import statements in __init__.py as follows −

```
from Pots import Pots
from Isdn import Isdn
from G3 import G3
```

After you add these lines to __init__.py, you have all of these classes available when you import the Phone package.

```
#!/usr/bin/python
# Now import your Phone Package.
import Phone

Phone.Pots()
Phone.Isdn()
Phone.G3()
```

126

When the above code is executed, it produces the following result –

```
I'm Pots Phone
I'm 3G Phone
I'm ISDN Phone
```

In the above example, we have taken example of a single functions in each file, but you can keep multiple functions in your files. You can also define different Python classes in those files and then you can create your packages out of those classes.

Python - Files I/O

This chapter covers all the basic I/O functions available in Python. For more functions, please refer to standard Python documentation.

Printing to the Screen

The simplest way to produce output is using the *print* statement where you can pass zero or more expressions separated by commas. This function converts the expressions you pass into a string and writes the result to standard output as follows —

```
#!/usr/bin/python
```

```
print "Python is really a great language,", "isn't it?"
```

This produces the following result on your standard screen —

```
Python is really a great language, isn't it?
```

Reading Keyboard Input

Python provides two built-in functions to read a line of text from standard input, which by default comes from the keyboard. These functions are —

- raw_input
- input

THE *RAW_INPUT* FUNCTION

The *raw_input([prompt])* function reads one line from standard input and returns it as a string (removing the trailing newline).

```
#!/usr/bin/python
```

```
str = raw_input("Enter your input: ");
print "Received input is : ", str
```

This prompts you to enter any string and it would display same string on the screen. When I typed "Hello Python!", its output is like this –

```
Enter your input: Hello Python
Received input is :  Hello Python
```

THE *INPUT* FUNCTION

The *input([prompt])* function is equivalent to raw_input, except that it assumes the input is a valid Python expression and returns the evaluated result to you.

```
#!/usr/bin/python
```

```
str = input("Enter your input: ");
print "Received input is : ", str
```

This would produce the following result against the entered input –

```
Enter your input: [x*5 for x in range(2,10,2)]
Recieved input is :  [10, 20, 30, 40]
```

Opening and Closing Files

Until now, you have been reading and writing to the standard input and output. Now, we will see how to use actual data files.

Python provides basic functions and methods necessary to manipulate files by default. You can do most of the file manipulation using a file object.

The *OPEN* Function

Before you can read or write a file, you have to open it using Python's built-in *open()* function. This function creates a file object, which would be utilized to call other support methods associated with it.

Syntax

```
file object = open(file_name [, access_mode][, buffering])
```

Here are parameter details —

- file_name — The file_name argument is a string value that contains the name of the file that you want to access.

- access_mode — The access_mode determines the mode in which the file has to be opened, i.e., read, write, append, etc. A complete list of possible values is given below in the table. This is optional parameter and the default file access mode is read (r).

buffering — If the buffering value is set to 0, no buffering takes place. If the buffering value is 1, line buffering is performed while accessing a file. If you specify the buffering value as an integer greater than 1, then buffering action is performed with the indicated buffer size. If negative, the buffer size is the system default(default behavior).

Here is a list of the different modes of opening a file —

Sr.No.	Modes & Description
1	**r** Opens a file for reading only. The file pointer is placed at the beginning of the file. This is the default mode.
2	**rb** Opens a file for reading only in binary format. The file pointer is placed at the beginning of the file. This is the default mode.
3	**r+** Opens a file for both reading and writing. The file pointer placed at the beginning of the file.
4	**rb+** Opens a file for both reading and writing in binary format. The file pointer placed at the beginning of the file.
5	**w** Opens a file for writing only. Overwrites the file if the file exists. If the file does not exist, creates a new file for writing.

6	**wb**
	Opens a file for writing only in binary format. Overwrites the file if the file exists. If the file does not exist, creates a new file for writing.
7	**w+**
	Opens a file for both writing and reading. Overwrites the existing file if the file exists. If the file does not exist, creates a new file for reading and writing.
8	**wb+**
	Opens a file for both writing and reading in binary format. Overwrites the existing file if the file exists. If the file does not exist, creates a new file for reading and writing.
9	**a**
	Opens a file for appending. The file pointer is at the end of the file if the file exists. That is, the file is in the append mode. If the file does not exist, it creates a new file for writing.

10	**ab**

Opens a file for appending in binary format. The file pointer is at the end of the file if the file exists. That is, the file is in the append mode. If the file does not exist, it creates a new file for writing.

11	**a+**

Opens a file for both appending and reading. The file pointer is at the end of the file if the file exists. The file opens in the append mode. If the file does not exist, it creates a new file for reading and writing.

12	**ab+**

Opens a file for both appending and reading in binary format. The file pointer is at the end of the file if the file exists. The file opens in the append mode. If the file does not exist, it creates a new file for reading and writing.

THE *FILE* OBJECT ATTRIBUTES

Once a file is opened and you have one *file* object, you can get various information related to that file.

Here is a list of all attributes related to file object –

Sr.No.	Attribute & Description
1	**file.closed** Returns true if file is closed, false otherwise.
2	**file.mode** Returns access mode with which file was opened.
3	**file.name** Returns name of the file.
4	**file.softspace** Returns false if space explicitly required with print, true otherwise.

EXAMPLE

```
#!/usr/bin/python

# Open a file
fo = open("foo.txt", "wb")
print "Name of the file: ", fo.name
print "Closed or not : ", fo.closed
print "Opening mode : ", fo.mode
print "Softspace flag : ", fo.softspace
```

This produces the following result −

```
Name of the file:  foo.txt
Closed or not :  False
Opening mode :  wb
Softspace flag :  0
```

THE *CLOSE()* METHOD

The close() method of a *file* object flushes any unwritten information and closes the file object, after which no more writing can be done.

Python automatically closes a file when the reference object of a file is reassigned to another file. It is a good practice to use the close() method to close a file.

SYNTAX

```
fileObject.close();
```

EXAMPLE

```
#!/usr/bin/python

# Open a file
fo = open("foo.txt", "wb")
print "Name of the file: ", fo.name
```

```
# Close opend file
fo.close()
```

This produces the following result −

```
Name of the file:  foo.txt
```

READING AND WRITING FILES

The *file* object provides a set of access methods to make our lives easier. We would see how to use *read()* and *write()* methods to read and write files.

THE *WRITE()* METHOD

The *write()* method writes any string to an open file. It is important to note that Python strings can have binary data and not just text.

The write() method does not add a newline character ('\n') to the end of the string −

SYNTAX

```
fileObject.write(string);
```

Here, passed parameter is the content to be written into the opened file.

EXAMPLE

```
#!/usr/bin/python

# Open a file
fo = open("foo.txt", "wb")
fo.write( "Python is a great language.\nYeah its great!!\n");
```

```
# Close opend file
fo.close()
```

The above method would create *foo.txt* file and would write given content in that file and finally it would close that file. If you would open this file, it would have following content.

```
Python is a great language.
Yeah its great!!
```

THE *READ()* METHOD

The *read()* method reads a string from an open file. It is important to note that Python strings can have binary data. apart from text data.

SYNTAX

```
fileObject.read([count]);
```

Here, passed parameter is the number of bytes to be read from the opened file. This method starts reading from the beginning of the file and if *count* is missing, then it tries to read as much as possible, maybe until the end of file.

EXAMPLE

Let's take a file *foo.txt*, which we created above.

```
#!/usr/bin/python

# Open a file
fo = open("foo.txt", "r+")
str = fo.read(10);
print "Read String is : ", str
# Close opend file
fo.close()
```

This produces the following result −

```
Read String is :  Python is
```

FILE POSITIONS

The *tell()* method tells you the current position within the file; in other words, the next read or write will occur at that many bytes from the beginning of the file.

The *seek(offset[, from])* method changes the current file position. The *offset*argument indicates the number of bytes to be moved. The *from* argument specifies the reference position from where the bytes are to be moved.

If *from* is set to 0, it means use the beginning of the file as the reference position and 1 means use the current position as the reference position and if it is set to 2 then the end of the file would be taken as the reference position.

EXAMPLE

Let us take a file *foo.txt*, which we created above.

```
#!/usr/bin/python

# Open a file
fo = open("foo.txt", "r+")
str = fo.read(10);
print "Read String is : ", str

# Check current position
position = fo.tell();
print "Current file position : ", position

# Reposition pointer at the beginning once again
position = fo.seek(0, 0);
```

```
str = fo.read(10);
print "Again read String is : ", str
# Close opend file
fo.close()
```

This produces the following result −

```
Read String is :  Python is
Current file position :  10
Again read String is :  Python is
```

RENAMING AND DELETING FILES

Python os module provides methods that help you perform file-processing operations, such as renaming and deleting files.

To use this module you need to import it first and then you can call any related functions.

THE RENAME() METHOD

The *rename()* method takes two arguments, the current filename and the new filename.

SYNTAX

```
os.rename(current_file_name, new_file_name)
```

EXAMPLE

Following is the example to rename an existing file *test1.txt* −

```
#!/usr/bin/python
import os
```

```
# Rename a file from test1.txt to test2.txt
os.rename( "test1.txt", "test2.txt" )
```

THE *REMOVE()* METHOD

You can use the *remove()* method to delete files by supplying the name of the file to be deleted as the argument.

SYNTAX

```
os.remove(file_name)
```

EXAMPLE

Following is the example to delete an existing file *test2.txt* –

```
#!/usr/bin/python
import os

# Delete file test2.txt
os.remove("text2.txt")
```

DIRECTORIES IN PYTHON

All files are contained within various directories, and Python has no problem handling these too. The os module has several methods that help you create, remove, and change directories.

The *MKDIR()* Method

You can use the *mkdir()* method of the os module to create directories in the current directory. You need to supply an argument to this method which contains the name of the directory to be created.

Syntax

```
os.mkdir("newdir")
```

Example

Following is the example to create a directory *test* in the current directory –

```
#!/usr/bin/python
import os

# Create a directory "test"
os.mkdir("test")
```

The *CHDIR()* Method

You can use the *chdir()* method to change the current directory. The chdir() method takes an argument, which is the name of the directory that you want to make the current directory.

Syntax

```
os.chdir("newdir")
```

Example

Following is the example to go into "/home/newdir" directory —

```
#!/usr/bin/python
import os
```

```
# Changing a directory to "/home/newdir"
os.chdir("/home/newdir")
```

THE *GETCWD()* METHOD

The *getcwd()* method displays the current working directory.

SYNTAX

```
os.getcwd()
```

EXAMPLE

Following is the example to give current directory —

```
#!/usr/bin/python
import os

# This would give location of the current directory
os.getcwd()
```

THE *RMDIR()* METHOD

The *rmdir()* method deletes the directory, which is passed as an argument in the method.

Before removing a directory, all the contents in it should be removed.

SYNTAX

```
os.rmdir('dirname')
```

EXAMPLE

Following is the example to remove "/tmp/test" directory. It is required to give fully qualified name of the directory, otherwise it would search for that directory in the current directory.

```
#!/usr/bin/python
import os

# This would  remove "/tmp/test"  directory.
os.rmdir( "/tmp/test"  )
```

FILE & DIRECTORY RELATED METHODS

There are three important sources, which provide a wide range of utility methods to handle and manipulate files & directories on Windows and Unix operating systems. They are as follows —

- File Object Methods: The *file* object provides functions to manipulate files.

- OS Object Methods: This provides methods to process files as well as directories.

PYTHON - EXCEPTIONS HANDLING

Python provides two very important features to handle any unexpected error in your Python programs and to add debugging capabilities in them –

- Exception Handling – This would be covered in this tutorial. Here is a list standard Exceptions available in Python: Standard Exceptions.

- Assertions – This would be covered in Assertions in Pythontutorial.

List of Standard Exceptions –

Sr.No.	Exception Name & Description
1	**Exception** Base class for all exceptions
2	**StopIteration** Raised when the next() method of an iterator does not point to any object.
3	**SystemExit** Raised by the sys.exit() function.

4	StandardError
	Base class for all built-in exceptions except StopIteration and SystemExit.

5	ArithmeticError
	Base class for all errors that occur for numeric calculation.

6	OverflowError
	Raised when a calculation exceeds maximum limit for a numeric type.

7	FloatingPointError
	Raised when a floating point calculation fails.

8	ZeroDivisionError
	Raised when division or modulo by zero takes place for all numeric types.

9	AssertionError
	Raised in case of failure of the Assert statement.

10	AttributeError Raised in case of failure of attribute reference or assignment.
11	EOFError Raised when there is no input from either the raw_input() or input() function and the end of file is reached.
12	ImportError Raised when an import statement fails.
13	KeyboardInterrupt Raised when the user interrupts program execution, usually by pressing Ctrl+c.
14	LookupError Base class for all lookup errors.
15	IndexError Raised when an index is not found in a sequence.

16   KeyError

Raised when the specified key is not found in the dictionary.

17   NameError

Raised when an identifier is not found in the local or global namespace.

18   UnboundLocalError

Raised when trying to access a local variable in a function or method but no value has been assigned to it.

19   EnvironmentError

Base class for all exceptions that occur outside the Python environment.

20   IOError

Raised when an input/ output operation fails, such as the print statement or the open() function when trying to open a file that does not exist.

21	IOError
	Raised for operating system-related errors.
22	SyntaxError
	Raised when there is an error in Python syntax.
23	IndentationError
	Raised when indentation is not specified properly.
24	SystemError
	Raised when the interpreter finds an internal problem, but when this error is encountered the Python interpreter does not exit.
25	SystemExit
	Raised when Python interpreter is quit by using the sys.exit() function. If not handled in the code, causes the interpreter to exit.
26	TypeError
	Raised when an operation or function is attempted that is invalid for the specified data type.

| 27 | ValueError |
| | Raised when the built-in function for a data type has the valid type of arguments, but the arguments have invalid values specified. |

| 28 | RuntimeError |
| | Raised when a generated error does not fall into any category. |

| 29 | NotImplementedError |
| | Raised when an abstract method that needs to be implemented in an inherited class is not actually implemented. |

ASSERTIONS IN PYTHON

An assertion is a sanity-check that you can turn on or turn off when you are done with your testing of the program.

The easiest way to think of an assertion is to liken it to a raise-if statement (or to be more accurate, a raise-if-not statement). An expression is tested, and if the result comes up false, an exception is raised.

Assertions are carried out by the assert statement, the newest keyword to Python, introduced in version 1.5.

Programmers often place assertions at the start of a function to check for valid input, and after a function call to check for valid output.

THE ASSERT STATEMENT

When it encounters an assert statement, Python evaluates the accompanying expression, which is hopefully true. If the expression is false, Python raises an *AssertionError* exception.

The syntax for assert is –

```
assert Expression[, Arguments]
```

If the assertion fails, Python uses ArgumentExpression as the argument for the AssertionError. AssertionError exceptions can be caught and handled like any other exception using the try-except statement, but if not handled, they will terminate the program and produce a traceback.

EXAMPLE

Here is a function that converts a temperature from degrees Kelvin to degrees Fahrenheit. Since zero degrees Kelvin is as cold as it gets, the function bails out if it sees a negative temperature –

```
#!/usr/bin/python
def KelvinToFahrenheit(Temperature):
    assert (Temperature >= 0),"Colder than absolute zero!"
    return ((Temperature-273)*1.8)+32
print KelvinToFahrenheit(273)
print int(KelvinToFahrenheit(505.78))
print KelvinToFahrenheit(-5)
```

When the above code is executed, it produces the following result –

```
32.0
451
Traceback (most recent call last):
File "test.py", line 9, in <module>
print KelvinToFahrenheit(-5)
File "test.py", line 4, in KelvinToFahrenheit
assert (Temperature >= 0),"Colder than absolute zero!"
AssertionError: Colder than absolute zero!
```

What is Exception?

An exception is an event, which occurs during the execution of a program that disrupts the normal flow of the program's instructions. In general, when a Python script encounters a situation that it cannot cope with, it raises an exception. An exception is a Python object that represents an error.

When a Python script raises an exception, it must either handle the exception immediately otherwise it terminates and quits.

Handling an exception

If you have some *suspicious* code that may raise an exception, you can defend your program by placing the suspicious code in a try: block. After the try: block, include an except: statement, followed by a block of code which handles the problem as elegantly as possible.

Syntax

Here is simple syntax of *try....except...else* blocks –

```
try:
    You do your operations here;
    .....................
except ExceptionI:
    If there is ExceptionI, then execute this block.
except ExceptionII:
    If there is ExceptionII, then execute this block.
    .....................
else:
    If there is no exception then execute this block.
```

Here are few important points about the above-mentioned syntax −

- A single try statement can have multiple except statements. This is useful when the try block contains statements that may throw different types of exceptions.

- You can also provide a generic except clause, which handles any exception.

- After the except clause(s), you can include an else-clause. The code in the else-block executes if the code in the try: block does not raise an exception.

- The else-block is a good place for code that does not need the try: block's protection.

EXAMPLE

This example opens a file, writes content in the, file and comes out gracefully because there is no problem at all −

```
#!/usr/bin/python

try:
    fh = open("testfile", "w")
    fh.write("This is my test file for exception handling!!")
except IOError:
    print "Error: can\'t find file or read data"
else:
    print "Written content in the file successfully"
    fh.close()
```

This produces the following result −

```
Written content in the file successfully
```

EXAMPLE

This example tries to open a file where you do not have write permission, so it raises an exception −

```
#!/usr/bin/python

try:
    fh = open("testfile", "r")
    fh.write("This is my test file for exception handling!!")
except IOError:
    print "Error: can\'t find file or read data"
else:
    print "Written content in the file successfully"
```

This produces the following result −

```
Error: can't find file or read data
```

THE *EXCEPT* CLAUSE WITH NO EXCEPTIONS

You can also use the except statement with no exceptions defined as follows −

```
try:
    You do your operations here;
    .....................
except:
    If there is any exception, then execute this block.
    .....................
else:
    If there is no exception then execute this block.
```

This kind of a try-except statement catches all the exceptions that occur. Using this kind of try-except statement is not considered a good programming practice though, because it catches all exceptions but does not make the programmer identify the root cause of the problem that may occur.

The *except* Clause with Multiple Exceptions

You can also use the same *except* statement to handle multiple exceptions as follows —

```
try:
    You do your operations here;
    .....................
except(Exception1[, Exception2[,...ExceptionN]]]):
    If there is any exception from the given exception list,
    then execute this block.
    .....................
else:
    If there is no exception then execute this block.
```

The try-finally Clause

You can use a finally: block along with a try: block. The finally block is a place to put any code that must execute, whether the try-block raised an exception or not. The syntax of the try-finally statement is this —

```
try:
    You do your operations here;
    .....................
    Due to any exception, this may be skipped.
finally:
    This would always be executed.
    .....................
```

You cannot use *else* clause as well along with a finally clause.

EXAMPLE

```
#!/usr/bin/python

try:
   fh = open("testfile", "w")
   fh.write("This is my test file for exception handling!!")
finally:
   print "Error: can\'t find file or read data"
```

If you do not have permission to open the file in writing mode, then this will produce the following result –

```
Error: can't find file or read data
```

Same example can be written more cleanly as follows –

```
#!/usr/bin/python

try:
   fh = open("testfile", "w")
   try:
      fh.write("This is my test file for exception handling!!")
   finally:
      print "Going to close the file"
      fh.close()
except IOError:
   print "Error: can\'t find file or read data"
```

When an exception is thrown in the *try* block, the execution immediately passes to the *finally* block. After all the statements in the *finally* block are executed, the exception is raised again and is handled in the *except*statements if present in the next higher layer of the *try-except* statement.

ARGUMENT OF AN EXCEPTION

An exception can have an *argument*, which is a value that gives additional information about the problem. The contents of the argument vary by exception. You capture an exception's argument by supplying a variable in the except clause as follows –

```
try:
    You do your operations here;
    ....................
except ExceptionType, Argument:
    You can print value of Argument here...
```

If you write the code to handle a single exception, you can have a variable follow the name of the exception in the except statement. If you are trapping multiple exceptions, you can have a variable follow the tuple of the exception.

This variable receives the value of the exception mostly containing the cause of the exception. The variable can receive a single value or multiple values in the form of a tuple. This tuple usually contains the error string, the error number, and an error location.

EXAMPLE

Following is an example for a single exception –

```
#!/usr/bin/python

# Define a function here.
def temp_convert(var):
    try:
        return int(var)
    except ValueError, Argument:
        print "The argument does not contain numbers\n", Argument
```

```
# Call above function here.
temp_convert("xyz");
```

This produces the following result —

```
The argument does not contain numbers
invalid literal for int() with base 10: 'xyz'
```

RAISING AN EXCEPTIONS

You can raise exceptions in several ways by using the raise statement. The general syntax for the raise statement is as follows.

SYNTAX

```
raise [Exception [, args [, traceback]]]
```

Here, *Exception* is the type of exception (for example, NameError) and *argument* is a value for the exception argument. The argument is optional; if not supplied, the exception argument is None.

The final argument, traceback, is also optional (and rarely used in practice), and if present, is the traceback object used for the exception.

EXAMPLE

An exception can be a string, a class or an object. Most of the exceptions that the Python core raises are classes, with an argument that is an instance of the class. Defining new exceptions is quite easy and can be done as follows —

```
def functionName( level ):
    if level < 1:
        raise "Invalid level!", level
        # The code below to this would not be executed
        # if we raise the exception
```

Note: In order to catch an exception, an "except" clause must refer to the same exception thrown either class object or simple string. For example, to capture above exception, we must write the except clause as follows –

```
try:
    Business Logic here...
except "Invalid level!":
    Exception handling here...
else:
    Rest of the code here...
```

USER-DEFINED EXCEPTIONS

Python also allows you to create your own exceptions by deriving classes from the standard built-in exceptions.

Here is an example related to *RuntimeError*. Here, a class is created that is subclassed from *RuntimeError*. This is useful when you need to display more specific information when an exception is caught.

In the try block, the user-defined exception is raised and caught in the except block. The variable e is used to create an instance of the class *Networkerror*.

```
class Networkerror(RuntimeError):
    def __init__(self, arg):
        self.args = arg
```

So once you defined above class, you can raise the exception as follows –

```
try:
    raise Networkerror("Bad hostname")
except Networkerror,e:
    print e.args
```

www.ingramcontent.com/pod-product-compliance
Lightning Source LLC
Chambersburg PA
CBHW071129050326
40690CB00008B/1400